WICKFORD
A History

J. Green & Son's employees outside their premises in Swan Lane, *c*.1930.

WICKFORD
A History

Judith Williams

Phillimore

2006

Published by
PHILLIMORE & CO. LTD
Shopwyke Manor Barn, Chichester, West Sussex, England
www.phillimore.co.uk

ISBN 1-86077-382-6
ISBN 13 978-1-86077-382-2

Printed and bound in Great Britain by
CAMBRIDGE PRINTING

To
Trevor Williams, Barrie Adcock
and Christopher Corbin

Contents

❖

List of Illustrations

Frontispiece: J. Green & Son's employees outside their premises in Swan Lane, *c.*1930

Acknowledgements

❖

I would like to thank the following organisations and individuals for permission to reproduce photographs: Phillimore & Co. Ltd 1; Southend Museums Service 3, 4, 5, 9, 94, 105, 111, 114, 115, 120, 121, 122, 123, 125, 147; Essex Record Office 8, 16, 19, 25, 33, 35, 56, 61, 71, 72, 83, 86, 95, 96, 110, 116, 124, 128, 142, 144, 145, 146; John Selby 14, 137; Christopher Corbin 20, 21, 26, 69, 89; Timothy Clement 32; Wickford Library collection 34, 38, 42, 75, 165; Tom Mayhew 40; www.footstepsphotos.co.uk 41, 44, 62, 98, 132; Barrie Adcock 48, 149, 159; Trevor Williams frontispiece, 49, 152, 155, 156, 157, 158; Essex Police Museum 76; Wickford police archives 87, 92, 97, 150, 151; Real Photographs Co. Ltd 102; Museum of English Rural Life, The University of Reading 126; Bell's Photo Co. Ltd 154; Edward Clack 164.

All other photographs are from the author's own collection. Every effort has been made to trace the copyright holders of photographs; I apologise for any omissions.

Thanks are due to the staff of Essex Record Office, Wickford Library, Chelmsford Library, Colchester Library, Southend Central Museum and the Museum of English Rural Life at the University of Reading. Also to the Rev. Philip Kearns for permission to take photographs in St Catherine's church.

In addition, I would particularly like to thank the following individuals for giving their time, imparting their knowledge, and making this book much more interesting, detailed and accurate than it otherwise would have been: Trevor Williams, Christopher Corbin, Barrie Adcock, Jo Cullen, Geoff Whiter, Tom Mayhew, Colin McGowan and Ken Crowe.

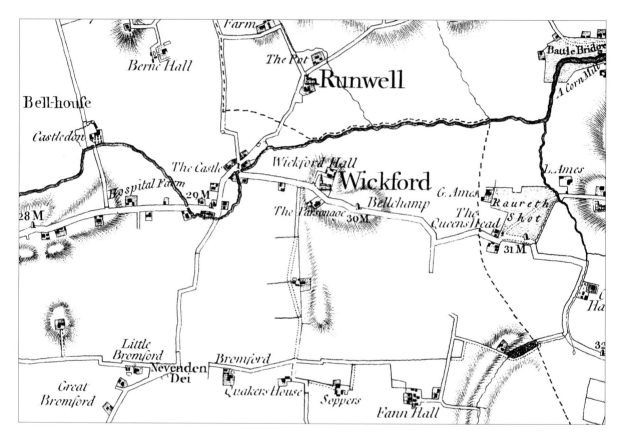

1 Chapman & André's map of 1777 showing Wickford's main buildings.

One

Neolithic to Normans

The town of Wickford stands at the head of the River Crouch in south-east Essex and can boast a long history as a site of settlement. Although the name 'Wickford', the sheep farm by the river crossing, suggests a Saxon settlement, both Iron-Age and Bronze-Age artefacts have been uncovered within the bounds of the current town, indicating that the site was settled long before the Saxons reached the area. It is likely that travellers used the easily forded crossing point on the River Crouch from prehistoric times.

Stone-Age flints and axe heads have been discovered locally. Bronze-Age axes have been found near the River Crouch at Wickford, while Bronze-Age pottery was uncovered at Shotgate Farm. Middle Iron-Age stockades, roundhouses and cremation burials were discovered along the route of the new A130, while remains of a late Iron-Age farming community, pottery, bowls and coins have been found at Barn Hall and in the area of Hilltop Junior School.

Britons

The first identifiable settlers in the area were members of the Trinovantes tribe of Britons who, before the Roman invasion in A.D. 43, held most of what is now the county of Essex. This tribe may have established a stronghold at Wickford, where the River Crouch was much wider than today and small boats could venture right into the village. Ten cremation pits were unearthed at Beauchamps Farm, suggesting a settlement of a considerable size. The Trinovantes and Romans were known to

have co-operated in a relationship based on trade of local goods in return for protection against the rival Catuvellauni tribe to the west, and Britons and Romans may have co-existed on the site of Wickford for a short while.

Some think that the location of the church and nearby moat (formerly adjacent to the rectory) suggests a site that was used for Celtic rituals.

Romans

The earliest evidence of Roman activity in the area is a small Roman fort, discovered in 1971 by the river and thought to be an early 'marching fort', used as a temporary stop-over on route marches during the first wave of Roman incursions into Britain.

Of greater significance, however, is the Iron-Age/Roman villa-farm (dating from *c.*A.D. 100) excavated in 1966-8, covering some 25-30 acres between the River Crouch and what is now Beauchamps High School. The villa would have been a self-contained community, with the family and their employees living together within an enclosure with their horses, cattle, sheep and pigs.

Evidence indicates a massive enclosure, surrounded by a ditch, in some sections as much as 30ft wide and 14ft deep. The main entrance to the enclosure faced east and another, smaller entry, thought to be the route cattle were driven to graze on the marshy banks of the Crouch, faced north. Within the enclosure were several stone and timber Roman buildings,

2 The River Crouch at Wickford Bridge. Wickford is named after the early river crossing near this point. Until Saxon times, the river was deep enough for small boats to travel right into the village centre.

both domestic and agricultural, including a 70ft long granary and a corn-drying oven.

A large grain storage pit, 16ft in diameter by 6ft deep, probably began as a clay mining

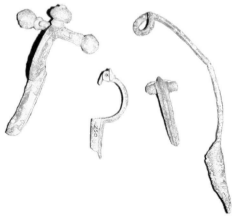

3 Roman jewellery found near the site of Beauchamps High School.

pit, the clay being used in the buildings. A ramp was cut for access to the grain and the interior of the pit was lined with woven basketwork and protected by a thatched roof. Excavation unearthed much carbonised grain while the wicker lining had turned to charcoal, suggesting that the pit had been a victim of fire occurring sometime between A.D. 170-200. About this time, the first scheme of defensive ditches around the site was abandoned and a second ditch was dug outside the first – this expansion indicates a period of prosperity for the residents.

The main building within the enclosure, a villa, had heating flues and a tiled roof; one tile having the impression of a Christian symbol, an alpha-omega motif, on it. Also found were several blue-painted timber planks that had been preserved in a waterlogged ditch, along with

4 Samian-ware pots such as this indicate that the Romans who lived at Wickford were wealthy.

5 Roman domestic pottery found at Wickford.

three late-Roman pedestal pots containing blue, white and red pigment. Domestic and personal items included glass, coins, ivory pins, a shale bracelet, pewter plate, a ring, bronze bracelets, combs, brooches, glass beads as well as coins, a small statuette of Venus and a skeleton of a dog. There were also fragments from glass bottles or windows, rusty nails, animal bones and oyster shells.

Some pottery finds had originated in Rettendon's Roman kilns; others were high quality Samian ware made in France or Germany, suggesting that the occupiers of Wickford's villa were wealthy people who enjoyed a high standard of living. In all, nearly 1½ tons of pottery and over 300 coins have been excavated from the site.

A 16ft deep, 3ft square, well was also excavated. This was found to have been lined with 2in-thick oak boards, and had wooden rungs fitted across the corners to act as a ladder, while the bottom of the well was lined with chalk. The lower half of the well was below the water table and, therefore, its contents were well-preserved. Objects found in the well include a wooden comb, a bobbin, a bucket, some decorated leather shoes and a small pewter dish with the name 'Amatius' on the bottom.

The smaller road crossing the north side of the enclosure ditch was probably just a track used to take the cattle across to graze on the marshes, while the road leading east from the villa was metalled and 15ft wide, with a flint kerb and side ditches. There was probably a Roman road connecting Wickford with South Benfleet and Canvey Island, where tiles and salt were produced, and roads may well have connected with Billericay and Bradwell.

The site continued to be farmed until a disastrous fire broke out towards the end of the fourth century destroying both the Roman villa and the farm buildings, and the site was abandoned. Subsequently, the area was cleared by Saxons wishing to use the site for their own purposes and much of the debris left by the fire was thrown into a ditch. Remaining Roman stone was looted by later settlers in the area for use in other building projects.

Saxons

After the Romans, Saxon settlers also identified the location as a convenient settlement point. It is they who left a permanent reminder of their settlement, not only in the local place-names such as Runweolla (Runwell) 'meeting place at a stream' and Haneghefelda (Hanningfield) 'the field of Hana's people', but also in the county

6 This cottage, typical of 16th-century rural Essex, stood at the south end of Wickford High Street, facing south. It survived until the mid-20th century.

name: Essex, the kingdom of the East Saxons. At Wickford, early Saxon pottery has been found, as well as evidence of early fifth-century Saxon houses, including a turf-and-rubble building constructed from material previously used by the Romans.

As populations grew, the Saxons organised their lands into parishes for administrative purposes and the parish of Wickford is thought to have been formed as early as A.D. 668. Parishes in turn became grouped into 'Hundreds', so named, not from the number of parishes they contained, but from the number of important men in the area. These men, the 'hundred-men' or 'earldor-men', would meet regularly in the main town of the Hundred to deal with issues that affected them all, for example, crime or poverty. Wickford was part of the Barstable Hundred, the main town of which was Great Burstead. The name Barstable or Berdestapla means 'by a pole', indicating a meeting place. The Barstable Hundred, one of 20 in Essex, comprised 35 parishes.

The first recorded landowner in Wickford is Aelthelflaed, the wife of the Saxon king Edmund. She died some time between A.D. 975 and 990 and her will states that she left 10 hides of land in Wickford to her kinsman, Sibeth. A hide was an area of about 120 acres, the amount of land needed to support a family (its exact size varied with the soil conditions). Aelthelflaed left other estates to her sister, Aelflaed, and to Brihtnoth, an Ealdorman of the East Saxons.

During Edward the Confessor's reign, the parish of Wickford comprised 12 parcels of land, each held by one or more free landowners. Of these, four parcels of land were manors, each presided over by a 'Lord of the Manor' who would take responsibility for the tenants on his land in return for work on the home farm. The lords of the manors at Wickford were Edwin Groat who owned 60 acres, Leofstan with 95 acres, Dot with 105 acres and Godwin, a thegn of King Edward, who owned 1,200 acres, thought to be the same estate previously owned by Aelthelflaed. A thegn was someone who had received the grant of land from the king himself and was entitled to receive taxes from the villagers living on the land.

Normans

When the Normans invaded England in 1066, all 20 of Wickford's landowners were dispossessed of their lands, and Wickford became re-distributed among four Norman landowners. This pattern of land holdings is shown in the Domesday survey, completed in 1086 by William the Conqueror for taxation purposes. The record provides a snap-shot of life in Wickford (then recorded as Wicfort) at the time.

By far the wealthiest landlord was Suene, whose father, Robert Fitzwimarc, was a personal friend of William the Conqueror. Suene became owner of over 60 manors in Essex including

the largest of the Wickford manors, previously owned by Godwin. Although reduced in value from £16 to £9, and with woodland reduced in extent from 12 hides to six acres (perhaps the timber had been used to build nearby Rayleigh Castle), this estate remained the most valuable land holding in the parish. Twenty-nine sheep and goats had been replaced with 20 sheep but there were three, instead of two, beehives. The men, now smallholders rather than slaves, owned only four ploughs, rather than the six they held before 1066.

Suene also became owner of Dot's 105-acre manor, valued at £10, and let it out to William, the son of Odo, Bishop of Bayeux. In addition, Suene acquired a further 30 acres, valued at £5, that had belonged to a man named Godric, and let it to Maynard.

7 View up High Street, c.1905. This thatched cottage, actually two semi-detached homes, stood just north of the cottage in No.6. The building became Prentice's Cycle Shop in the early 1900s.

8 Nevendon Road, *c.*1890.

Furthermore, Suene took Leofstan's manor and amalgamated it with two parcels of land previously belonging to four freemen and another parcel of land formerly belonging to a freewoman, Bricteva. This manorial estate, now comprising about 224 acres, was tenanted for Suene by Thorkell.

Suene established his main seat in the county at nearby Rayleigh where he built a castle. Tenants and peasants living on Suene's Wickford lands would have benefited from the protection of the castle in return for allegiance to Suene. Wickford timber and labour may well have been used to strengthen the castle.

9 Melrose Cottage, Southend Road, Shotgate.

The second largest landholder in Wickford at the time was Odo, the Bishop of Bayeux and brother of William the Conqueror, who established his main seat at Great Burstead. Odo was in possession of 240 acres of Wickford land previously belonging to two freemen and which, at the time of the Domesday survey, he rented to Pointel and Osbern. The survey records that 'Ravengar took this land away from them [the Saxons]; now the English do not know how it came into the Bishop's hand'.

Odo's second parcel of land was 288 acres worth £40 and wrested from five freemen. This was tenanted by the son of a fellow Norman, Turold. Turold himself took part in the Battle of Hastings, is depicted on the Bayeux Tapestry, and is known to have been ruthless in his acquisition of land. At Hanningfield, for example, he usurped 22 freemen and took their lands.

In addition, Odo owned 120 acres of pasture and woodland, valued at £20, previously belonging to the freeman Godric and, in 1086, let to Teher.

The two other Wickford landholders at 1086 were Modwin, who had obtained the 60-acre manor from Edwin Groat, and Ilbod, who came to possess 40 acres of land previously held by two freemen.

In all, Wickford comprised about 2,000 acres of cultivated land at Domesday. The effects of the Norman Conquest were felt throughout the social scale and, although the wealthiest of Wickford lost the freehold right to their lands, several of the serfs (almost equivalent to slaves) became bordars under the new regime, being given a small patch of land and thus more responsibility for themselves, although still with few rights.

There were 11 more working men in the village in 1086 than at 1066, while the six named landowners had been replaced by four landowning lords and seven tenants under them. The tenants would have held the land by service, rather than a monetary rent. For example, for use of the land they would have been obliged to fight in the landlord's 'army' for a certain number of days a year.

10 Guinea Pig Hall on Runwell Road was part of the Stileman's Estate. Samuel Brunwin gave it for the use of ministers of the first Congregational Chapel, built opposite in 1811.

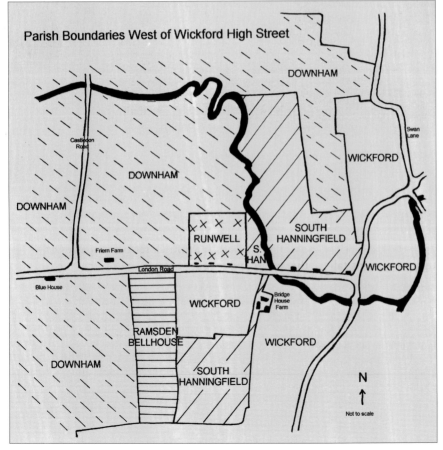

11 London Road and Ivy Cottage. This picture clearly demonstrates how the cottage got its name.

12 Parish boundaries map showing how land west of the High Street belonged to other parishes. The South Hanningfield fields became part of Wickford in 1888; most of the other fields shown joined Wickford in 1960.

13 The River Crouch and haystacks: a rural idyll at Wickford, c.1920.

The overall reduction in the number of pastoral animals in Wickford might indicate a shift to arable farming between the years 1066–1086, although the reduction in the number of plough animals suggests a slight fall in population, with less land being ploughed. Where comparisons of land values are given in Domesday Book, values seem to have fallen, possibly a result of the relative rise in importance of Rayleigh.

Although the Domesday survey only gives numbers of working men, the total population of the Wickford lands at 1086, including wives and children, was probably between 100 and 120 persons. In comparison, Billericay had a

population of about 400 people and Great Burstead, still the nominal 'chief town' of the Hundred, 100-200 people.

The north, south, and eastern boundaries of the parish were much the same as the town of Wickford today. However, most of the land west of the High Street, that is now part of Wickford, belonged to the parishes of Runwell, South Hanningfield and Downham. People living in this area would have paid taxes to the lords of the manors in those parishes and would not have appeared in any of the records relating to Wickford parish. Nevendon existed as a parish in its own right, while there was no settlement in the area that is now Shotgate.

Two
Early Development

Life for the population of Wickford revolved around the farming year and for four hundred years following the Norman Conquest the majority of men worked as agricultural labourers, with women and children helping in the fields where they could.

The Church

The first known church on the site of the present St Catherine's, the highest point in the parish, was built during the 12th century. It has been suggested that the church was built on a site of former Celtic rituals. In 1154, Robert of Essex, Suene's son, gave this church at Wickford to the priory of Prittlewell, which he had founded four years

14 There is known to have been a church on the site of St Catherine's since the 12th century. This sketch shows how the church looked when it was rebuilt in the 14th century.

previously. This meant that tithes from the parishioners of Wickford were given to the priory. St Catherine's was rebuilt in the 13th or 14th century with a wooden belfry and shingled spire and two bells made by John Kebyll, a London bell founder. One of the bells in the church tower dates from 1460 and bears the inscription 'Santa Katerina Ora Pro Nobis' (Saint Catherine, pray for us). This is the only evidence that the original church was dedicated to St Catherine. The slightly larger bell is inscribed 'Sit Nomen Domini Benedictum' (Blessed be the name of the Lord). Unlike the present St Catherine's, the 12th-century church had a gallery, which may well have been where musicians stood to accompany the service. The chancel roof was of 14th-century fine carved oak, which, legend says, was originally used in Prittlewell Priory refectory, and memorials in the church included a stone in the chancel engraved with the figures of three adults and eight children. St Catherine's remained attached to Prittlewell Priory until the dissolution of the monasteries by Henry VIII in 1539.

Adam de Stratton is the first known incumbent of St Catherine's, 1279-92, when he also held the livings of Black Notley, Bramfold and Hadleigh. Such 'pluralism' was frowned upon as, while the rector benefited from all the tithes, he was obviously resident in only one parish with the other parishes, as Wickford probably was in this case, left in charge of a curate. De Stratton was followed

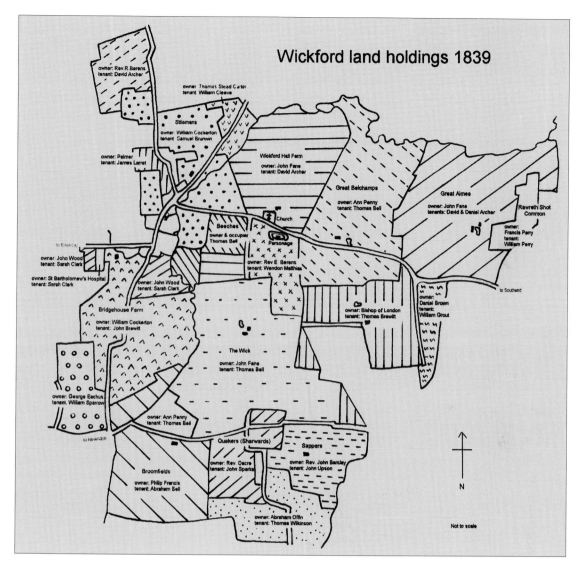

15 Map showing Wickford's farms, landowners and tenants in 1839. In 1557, the Wickford Hall Estate included over 20 dwellings.

by a man known simply as Petrus. This may have been the same person as Peter de Sandale, incumbent 1325-30.

John de Saracenis had been acting as rector for a year on 20 December 1311 when he was allowed an extension to remain in office for nine months while he became ordained. During his tenure, William de Norwyco of Stepelmoron, vicar of Wickford, was pardoned for causing the death of Adam, son of Ralph le Fevre of 'Wycheford', on 25 July 1311.

Wickford residents had trouble with neighbouring clerics also when John de Aynton, parson of Rayleigh, was found guilty of clipping coins (reducing their value) and his nephew, also John, was found guilty of violently assaulting John Beauchamp of Wickford in 1351.

16   Nevendon Bridge, *c.*1880. This area remained very rural right up until the 20th century.

Manors and landownership

By the 13th century the four manors within the bounds of Wickford indicated by the Domesday survey had become redistributed into only two large manorial sites: the manor of Wickford Hall and the manor of Stileman's. Possession of a manor and the role of Lord of the Manor entitled the owner to certain rights, for example, service or rent money from anyone living on the manor lands, fees from any markets or fairs on the land, and sometimes hunting rights in the woodlands.

The location of the manors resulted in the unusual situation at Wickford of the town centre developing separately from the parish church. The church was at Wickford Hall,

built on high ground in the tradition of early churches, while the town centre grew up around Stileman's manor house, close to the river, which was an important factor in the economic life of the village. Interestingly, the advowson, the right to appoint the incumbent of the church, was invested in the lord of the manor of Stileman's.

Wickford Hall

Wickford Hall stood between the present-day Southend Road and the River Crouch, behind St Catherine's church, within an estate of some 150 acres of mainly arable land. When Edward III confiscated the lands from Suene's grandson, Henry, Wickford Hall became a Crown possession until 1190 when Richard I granted the manor to Richard Ulric (also called Urry or Urric), Commander of the King's Crossbowmen.

In 1207, Richard Urric is recorded as holding 320 acres of land in Wickford, the work of the men of Wickford, 15 acres of mead, 12 acres of pasture and a windmill, as well as a grove of two acres and pasture for 280 sheep on Canewdon marsh. Urric died in 1247 leaving a wife, Marsilla, but the land became a joint possession of Isabel Urry and her sister, which some sources name as Maud, and others Matilda. Matilda married Martin Fitzsimon, while Isabel inherited the entire Wickford Estate, changing her name from Urry to de Wykeford. The produce of the mill was valued at 22s. 4d. per annum.

Isabel's grandson, Gilbert de Urry, held Wickford Manor until he died c.1300 and passed it to his son Nicholas, his grandson, also Nicholas, and great-grandson, Roland de Wykeford.

In 1460 the manor was held by Robert Plantagenet, Earl of Kent, and by the time

17 Wickford Hall, now converted into flats in Brunwin Close. As the landowners did not live in the parish, Wickford Hall spent its early life as the home of farmers, rather than lords.

Henry VIII came to the throne (1509) the manor belonged to Elizabeth Pound, her son William and his son, Anthony.

It then passed to Henry and Honora Radcliffe who sold to Arthur Harrys (Harris). In June 1561, James Harrys died at Wickford and willed five shillings to 'the poor men's box in Wickford', and to the poor of Rayleigh 20 shillings a year for three years. All his cows,

18 Stileman's farmhouse, Runwell Road. This five-bedroomed house was built about 1730, replacing the original manor house. It had two sitting rooms, a kitchen, dairy, coal and beer cellars, and an attic.

sheep, hogs, wheat, oats and his horse he left to his wife, Joan, but he left his house and lands to his brother, William Harrys.

Christopher Harris was the owner of Wickford Hall in 1566, following which the lands passed through the hands of Edward Harris to Sir William Harrys of Shenfield Place, Margaretting in 1603. At that time the estate included over 20 dwellings, most of which were tied cottages or were leased to labourers. Subsequently, it belonged to Edmund Godwin of Surrey and then to three generations of the Vaughan family. It was later rented and then sold to the Luther family and in the 19th century was in the possession of Colonel John Fane.

Stileman's

The second major estate in Wickford was the manor of Stileman's, comprising some 160 acres including fields which were officially part of Downham, South Hanningfield and Runwell parishes. By the Middle Ages, local justice, dealing with petty crime and disorder, was administered from the Court Leet held at the manor. An ancient pound, probably little more than a tiny shack, stood near the Stileman's manor house. While this would be the first stop for drunkards or vagrants, more serious criminals would have been taken to Chelmsford to be tried at the Quarter Sessions.

The name of the manor probably originates from its 15th-century owner, William Stuyleman, who purchased 31 acres of land in Wickford in 1488.

Another early owner was a Mr Batcher, who sold the estate to Richard Cupper of London for £280 in 1562. In 1650 the estate was in the hands of Robert Chester who passed it to his sister's son, John Moor. It descended to his son and grandson, both called Chester Moor.

Chester Moor jun. had no children and left the estate to his cousin John Hall who, in honour of his relatives, named his son and heir Chester Moor Hall. Chester Moor Hall

(1703-71) was born at Leigh and lived at Sutton near Southend. He became a King's Counsel and an inventor, notably of the achromatic telescope. He bequeathed Stileman's to his sister, Martha Hall of Brentwood. In her will, proved 4 December 1782, Martha provided that the appointment of the next rector of Wickford should be given to the Rev. Thomas Morrison, the rector of Sutton, in order that he himself could be 'duly and fully instituted and inducted therto'. However, Morrison never acquired the living, probably because the resident incumbent, Peter Beauvoir, retained his position for 61 years (1761-1822). Stileman's Farm, then occupied by James Punt, she left to her cousin William Cockerton of Sutton, who became one of Wickford's major landowners.

The original Stileman's manor house, described by D. Coller in 1861 as 'once a noble mansion', stood on the western side of what is now Wickford Broadway, north of Swan Lane, but was dismantled about 1730 and replaced by a larger timber-boarded construction.

For most of the 19th century, Stileman's was tenanted and then owned by the Brunwin family.

Farms

In addition to these two manors, early Wickford comprised nine minor farmsteads: Great Aimes, Little Aimes, Great Belchamps (later called Beauchamps), Beeches, The Wick, Broomfields, Quakers (also known as Sharwards), Sappers, and Bridge House.

Wick Farm, sometimes called The Wick, was originally a manor in its own right, but became part of Wickford Hall Manor when it was taken over by the same owners. With over 300 acres, it was the largest farm holding in Wickford, stretching from the present Russell Gardens south to Cranfield Park Road; it was bounded by a tributary of the River Crouch, now the site of the Nevendon Road by-pass in the west, nearly to the parish boundary,

19 View into town across Wickford Bridge, *c.*1890.

where Salcott Crescent now runs, in the east. The Mill Field adjacent to the River Crouch was part of this estate and was most likely the location of a watermill. The Wick farmhouse was rebuilt in the 17th century, but this burnt down in the 1960s. Occupiers in the early 18th century were Thomas Young, Giles Bacon and John Crouch, while the ownership passed through the Vaughan and Fane families.

Great Aimes and Little Aimes in the extreme east of the parish were purchased by the same landowner as early as 1700, and since that time were treated as one land holding. The estate, now known as Shot Farm, lay between the River Crouch and the Southend Road, and from where the Southminster branch of the railway line now runs to the boundary with Rawreth parish in the east. Archaeological finds show that the site was continuously occupied since the Bronze Age and that by the medieval period the residents were very wealthy. The estate was most probably one of the four manors listed in Domesday Book, but later became subservient to Wickford Hall.

The original name of the estate comes from William and John Ame, a father and son recorded living in Wickford in 1300. Roger Rede owned the land in about 1540, while in 1655 William Read was occupier of 'a tenement called Great Amyes' and 40 acres of land in Wickford for a yearly rent of £7. He also rented 12 acres of land called 'Little Amyes' at a yearly rent of £3 and six shillings.

In August 1687 a dispute arose over whether the Read family owned the copyhold rights to the land. The heirs of William Read issued a warrant dated 5 September 1693 for a bailiff to seize the land. However, it was decided that Read had sold the land as a freehold property and had not retained copyhold rights.

Sarah Western owned Great and Little Aimes in 1731 when the estate was described as 'a capital messuage with barn, stables and other outhouses'. It comprised 177 acres of land and a right of common on Rawreth Shot, together with seven and a half acres of arable land called Homefield Pightles, formerly part of Little Aimes, to which there belonged another

20 Ilgars farmhouse, Runwell Road. Ilgars, in Runwell parish adjacent to the church, was also known as Ilgoers or Drivers Farm, and its fields extended into Wickford parish.

right of common on Rawreth Shot. The estate included significant areas of oak and elm.

When Sir Thomas Mostyn purchased the farms, he was advised that Great and Little Aimes together were formerly let at a rent of £90 a year and could command a similar rent again after a little renovation. The farms had been much 'neglected and abused' by the previous two tenants; the landlord living at a great distance from it, he chose to reduce the rent rather than put up the money for improvements that he would not be able to oversee himself. Gabriel Cox had been granted a lease for 21 years from Michaelmas (29 September) 1737 at the yearly rent of £70 for the first four years, on account of Cox repairing the fences, which were in very bad condition, and at £85 per annum for the residue of the term. It was suggested to Sir Thomas that the fields would now benefit from a dressing of chalk, 'the carriage of which is very convenient by the river or creek which bounds the lands on one side'.

The land agent concluded that 'upon the whole, this estate is so improvable and is so convenient for the sending of its produce to London Market either by water or land carriage that it cannot be worth less than 26 years purchase at £100 p.a.'

The Luther and Fane families owned the estate in the 18th and 19th centuries when it comprised 191 acres of mainly arable. The names Great Aimes and Little Aimes disappeared in the 19th century when it was renamed Shot Farm, from its location adjacent to Rawreth Shot.

In January 1747, John Vaughan sold a field from the estate called Kings Mead, containing three and a half acres, for the sum of £44 to John Sharpe. Sharpe added the land to Cabes (or Caves), a farm on Rawreth Shot, and renamed the farm Shotgate. Daniel Brown, a tenant of the farm, took the opportunity to buy it and his grandson, Daniel Brown Grout, inherited it.

The site of Great Belchamps (Beauchamps) Farm was inhabited from Iron-Age times and, as mentioned in Chapter 1, is the location of interesting Iron-Age and Roman archaeological finds. The name of the farm is derived from the family of an early owner, John du Beauchamp of Shopland near Southend. The River Crouch marks the northern boundary of the farm, and the Southend Road its southern boundary; it stretched from what is now the Southminster railway branch line in the east to Highcliff Close in the west, covering nearly 200 acres. The farm was 'acknowledged to be of worse land than any other in the parish' according to the rector of 1822, who reduced the tithe payments accordingly.

In the early 17th century, Great Belchamps was tenanted by Vincent Sympson of Runwell. When he died in 1627, the land was divided between his daughters, Mary, wife of William Humphrey of Runwell, and Bridget, wife of Woodhall Streat of Runwell, with Bridget and her husband keeping the main house.

The deeds stipulated that, as per the will of Vincent Simpson, three shillings per year was to be paid out of the profits from the land to the poor of St Bartholomew's Hospital. In 1714, while occupied by Samuel Wolfe, Belchamps was conveyed to Jeremiah Gregory of Kent from Richard Moor for £1,685. The farm was inherited by Jeremiah's son and grandson, both named Edward Gregory, and in 1734 Edward Gregory was the only Wickford landowner to vote in the parliamentary elections. Beauchamps saw its last agricultural crop in 1965.

In the south-west corner of Wickford, as its name suggests, Bridge House Farm stood adjacent to the bridge over the Crouch on the London Road. The estate stretched from the London Road to Nevendon Tye and from where St Peter's Catholic church now stands to the Nevendon Road by-pass. It also included several fields belonging to South Hanningfield parish. The farm appears in records as early

21   Rear of Ilgars farmhouse, seen here just before it was demolished, c.1900.

22   Bromfords Farm in Nevendon included fields in Wickford parish.

as 1617 and was unusual in being farmed by its owner who, for much of the 18th century, was Thomas Howlett and, in the 19th, John Brewitt.

The original farmhouse was replaced by a brick building in the 19th century, with a slate roof. It had its own brewhouse, as well as two coachhouses, two large barns and a cart lodge.

Beeches Farm took its name from the Beche family who once lived there. The property was a compact estate south of the Southend Road and its farmers rented additional fields from other estates to increase their acreage.

23   Southend Road, with Beeches farmhouse seen in the distance on the right. Beeches was the home of the Bell family for many years.

24 Weather-boarded cottage in Swan Lane near the junction with Jersey Gardens.

Beeches' farmhouse was greatly extended in the 18th century by the then owner Thomas Bell, one of the first owner-occupiers in the parish.

Sappers Farm, in the south-east of the parish, takes its name from John Sopper who owned the lands in the 1340s. At various times the farm appears in records as Sapers, Soppers and Suppers, and it comprised eight fields with the farmhouse at the centre. During the 19th century the farm was owned by the Rev. John Barclay and tenanted by the Upson family. It was sold in the 1890s, divided into smallholding sites and, as such, escaped dense housing development.

Broomfields Farm in the south of the parish took its name from Hubert de Bromfield who owned the property in 1285. The Wickford portion of the farm was a square estate south of Cranfield Park Road, stretching from the present Lower Park Road to Newlands Road. Other fields lay within Nevendon parish. A new wattle and daub house replaced the original house in the 16th century and a further wing was added in the 17th century.

The small farm called Quakers, also known as Sharwards, covered some 50 acres on the road to North Benfleet, bounded on the north and east by what is now Cranfield Park Road. Newlands Road marks its western boundary and the Chase and Fairway its southern extent. In 1731 it was owned by Mr Birch and was one of the farms tenanted by Gabriel Cox. Around 1800 Jacob Cranfield was tenant farmer of Quakers, and in 1833 it was leased to John Sparks, a North Benfleet farmer. However, typically of leases of the time, the valuable trees and timber on the land was reserved for the owner, the Rev. William Dakins of Westminster, who also retained the right to hunt, shoot, fish, fowl and sport upon or over the said lands. Sparks was to pay £25 p.a. for the first two years, £47 for the next three years and £50 for the remaining nine years of the lease. At the end of the 19th century, Quakers was sold off and its lands became the smallholdings named Inyati, Barstable and Cotswold Farm.

Other land holdings in the parish included the glebe land, which extended to some 48 acres

25 Two terraces of weather-boarded cottages with the parish water pump between them, *c*.1915. The poster, far left, is calling for recruits to His Majesty's army. This area became the site of the Willowdale shopping centre.

south of the Southend Road and was rented out to supplement the rector's income.

Approximately 105 acres in the south east of the parish were part of the property associated with the position of the Bishop of London since *c*.A.D. 1100.

One small Wickford field on the London Road was part of Hospital Farm (later called Friern Farm), owned by the Governors of St Bartholomew's Hospital until the 20th century. The majority of this farm's fields were part of Downham parish. Rentals from the farm contributed to the expenses of the hospital and an additional fine was payable by the tenants if blood was shed on the land during Christmas, Easter or Whitsun weeks, or if a male bastard was born there.

Geldables

As well as the aforementioned farms, Wickford benefited from two geldables. Geldables are districts geographically within one parish but which officially belonged to a different one. The word geldable derives from the Saxon 'gyldan' to pay and, often, these areas paid taxes to both parishes.

One of Wickford's geldables was in Runwell and South Hanningfield, during the 18th century rated to the land tax at £98, and the other was part of the parish of Rawreth, rated at £134. Rawreth properties paying taxes of four shillings in the pound to Wickford included Cockertons, part of Burrels and part of Little Fanton Hall. Benton records that geldables were liable for 'the full king's tax and one third of the constable's rate'.

Rawreth Shot

Ten acres of the land known as Rawreth Shot was in the parish of Wickford, although most of it (32 acres) was in Rawreth parish. The word 'shot' derives from a Saxon word for a part or a portion, and was used in medieval times to describe an area of land divided into strips, each farmed by separate individuals.

Rawreth Shot became 'common ground', over which the owners of seven local houses held the right to use the land. In 1741 it was described as 'very good land' and the Enclosure Act of 1855 saw Rawreth Shot divided between private landowners.

Early landowners

When Alexander de Bertlesden died, *c*.1202, his wife Marsill let his estate in Wickford to her brother-in-law Richard de Bertlesden. In return, Richard granted her seven acres of land in the parish 'in the great field below the house which was of William le Geist towards the east to hold

as dower'. Richard was also to give Marsill one third of a mark of silver plus seven shillings and a horse-load of wheat each year.

After Marsill's death, the seven acres was to revert to her daughter Felicia to hold from Richard and his heirs by one pound of cumin seed a year (i.e. a nominal rent).

In 1231 Felicia, now married to William de Norfolk, owned 36 acres of land in 'Wycford', tenanted by William de Dercet. By 1242, 16 acres of Felicia de Wykeford's land, called Helewyseland, was owned by William Talebot, and was tenanted by Robert de Tytleshal and his wife Cecily, for 40 marks of silver.

William le Butiler rented 30 acres of land in Wickford to Andrew le Purte for one mark of silver in 1247.

26 St Mary's church, Runwell, seen here in a photograph taken by the then rector, the Rev. Henry Kingsford Harris, in about 1900, was completely refurbished in 1907. Note the roofline.

27 View of High Street, looking north. The white gates on the left mark the entrance to Dr Marshall's detached house, which stood in three acres of ground, extending behind the High Street. Dr Marshall was surgeon to Wickford parish for 48 years and is remembered in a stained glass window in St Catherine's.

In 1250, Robert le Noreys took on the tenancy of 15 acres of land at Wickford from William de Godel and Joan his wife. Le Noreys undertook to hold the 15 acres for one penny plus all service, suit of court, homage, relief, fealty aid, wardship, custom and exaction. This indicates the responsibilities that came with land ownership, and the delegation of these responsibilities was often more valuable than a rental income.

Local Concerns

In 1253, Billericay was granted a charter to hold a market and, soon afterwards, two annual fairs. An annual fair was also held at Basildon from about the same time and, as competition for the right to hold markets and fairs was prevalent among neighbouring landlords, this may explain why Wickford did not develop a market or fair of its own. These major events would have focused attention away from Wickford, and Billericay became the main commercial centre of the Barstable Hundred. Great Burstead, meanwhile, retained its position as the ecclesiastical centre of the area until the 19th century, despite its population being quickly overtaken by that of Billericay.

Lying in a natural depression between Billericay, Rayleigh, Hanningfield and Langdon Hills, the area around Wickford was known as the Mundon Trough. Its location on the River Crouch left the village open to regular flooding, exacerbated by the underlying London Clay soil. The Tithe Map of 1839 shows 19 plots of land marked 'not used', and flooding is

28 Delivery carts, High Street, *c.*1915. The sign in the garden on the left offers 'Freehold land for sale'.

probably the reason for this. However, in the early days of settlement, the marshy ground would have been used for grazing sheep in the summer and for hunting wildfowl, such as teal, shoveler, pochard and sheldrake, in the winter.

National Concerns

The Black Death in 1348 brought about a general decline in the population of Essex villages, killing almost half of the labourers on the land. It may be the reason that occupation of the site of Dollymans Farm suddenly ceased at this time. Cultivated fields returned to the

wild and manorial lords began to rent out fields. Leasehold land was created and a new type of farmer appeared, owning and living on his own land and employing peasants as landless labourers.

Rettendon, Downham and Billericay have all been recorded as active in the Peasants' Revolt of 1381, so it is more than likely that villagers from Wickford were also involved. When they realised their cause was lost, the peasants involved in the revolt fled to Norsey Wood, north of Billericay, where hundreds of them were hunted down and killed.

Three

The Tudor and Stuart Period

Wickford Residents

During Henry VIII's reign (1509-47), Wickford landowners are known to have included Robert Sharpe, Thomasine Hopton-alias-Louseworth, Richard Allen, Thomas Bonham, Levi Bell and Richard Wise. Joan Risson was a wealthy member of the community and when she wrote her will on 4 June 1567 she left her goods to her sons, daughters and grandchildren but also 'to the poor mens box of Wickford 3s. 4d.' and, not forgetting her dependants, 'to every servant in the house 12d apiece'.

The names of more humble members of the town can be found in the parish registers which

29 St Catherine's church. Between 1775 and 1812, 128 marriages took place at St Catherine's. Names occurring regularly in the registers include Tanner, Bugby, Reed, Salmon, Bell, Purkis, Adey and Swan.

date back to 1538, beginning with the baptism of John Midleton on 12 January, and the Muster Rolls of 1539. These lists were drawn up by Henry VIII, concerned that his disagreement with the Pope might induce an invasion of Britain from France or Germany, and comprise a list of all the men and their weapons in each Hundred. Together, the Barstable Hundred mustered 19 parsons, vicars and priests, '3 priests that be good bowmen', five gentlemen, 301 archers, 124 billmen (a bill being a large curved knife) and just one gunner (Edmund Redworth of South Benfleet).

In Wickford (Wygford) itself there were four 'bowmen', two of whom actually owned a bow, with 1,117 arrows between them. There were ten 'billmen' but only James Ryde, Thomas Gyles and Robert Smith owned a bill of their own. Richard Pon had his own dagger, while Roger Mode could offer a harness.

'Wygford Gyldable', the part of Wickford within Rawreth parish, could find six bowmen with 67 arrows. Only one of these, Robert Badon, owned a bow and, despite registering himself as an archer, John Derby owned a 'bill dagger'. Also among the archers was Thomas Corlew who owned 'a wepyn callyd an holywater synbyll'. This formidable weapon was, in fact, a heavy wooden club studded with iron spikes and took its name from a fancied resemblance to the vessels used to distribute holy water then in common use in churches. There were ten billmen in the geldable; two owned a dagger and Henry Stone had a share of a harness.

In addition to these fighting men were seven men listed as 'Dedwood: not able'. However, these men appear to have been better equipped than the able men. Perhaps they were older and thus had more accumulated wealth, for among them were two men with a bill and four with a harness, while William Pascall offered 'a hole harnes and a horse' for the service of his country.

30 This window in St Catherine's vestry is thought to date from the 15th century.

However, as eloquently explained by the *Essex Countryside* magazine, 'the expected invasion never materialized and Thomas Corlew was never called on to knock an invader on the head with his holy water sprinkler'.

Religious Matters

The Tudor period was one of religious unrest for the whole country and Wickford, along with much of south Essex, became known for its Puritan leanings. With each change of monarch members of the clergy were at risk of losing their livings or even their lives, depending on whether their views agreed with those of the state church.

Wickford, however, was fortunate in the stability of its clergy and, between 1456 and 1548, St Catherine's saw only six rectors, all of whom remained in office until their death.

In 1551, St Catherine's passed from the control of the Crown and the advowson (the right to appoint the priest) was given to the

RECTORS OF WICKFORD

1305	Petrus
1330	Hugh de Neels
1349	Henry de Chesterfield
1349	John de Kent
1349	William de Pellat
1351	Olivier de Halstede
	William de Tolse
1357	Thomas de Besewyke
1360	William de Ferribie
1364	William de Capel de Sapcote
	William Wright
1371	Galfridus Spede
1372	Robert de Sonning
	Robert Hele de Sprotton
1384	John Muriell
1396	William Person
1398	John atte Mell
1399	William Hale
	or William Welbys
1439	John Egiott
1446	John Dose
1450	Nicholas Gundall
1456	Michael Nicholson
1467	John Baron
1481	Richard Nelson
1512	Robert Offley
1546	John Tendring
1548	William Astonce
1551	Christopher Eton
1554	Ralph Byrch
	Christopher Eton
1561	Henry Wright
1572	John Taylor
1591	William Harries
1610	Augustine Lyndsell
1623	Richard Hayward
1624	Joshua Mapletoft
1635	Cornelius Gray
1647	Nicholas Bound
1661	Robert Percivall
1672	Richard Pulley
1677	John Pulley
1730	Thomas Case
1761	Peter Beauvoir
1822	Charles Atmore Ogilvie
1823	Richard Peter Whish
1827	Thomase Hulse
1833	Edward Rion Berens
1867	William Hugo Lukin
1881	James Lukin
1887	John Morley Trunian
1888	George Porter
1898	Herbert Lovaine Barrett Leonard
1899	Francis Dormer Pierce
1908	Wallace Bryant
1916	Henry Hook Bartrum
1920	Edward William Brereton
1924	James Talbot
1930	Constantine Philpot Koelle
1932	Arthur George Manson
1956	Robert d'Esterre Archdale Byrn
1962	Frederick Charles Victor Prance
1973	William Arthur Randall
1980	Arthur Roy Thomas
1986	David Walter Lowman
1994	Christine Ann McCafferty

31 The list of rectors of St Catherine's dates back to 1305, beginning with Petrus. Peter Beauvoir was Wickford's longest serving rector: 1761-1822.

32 Augustine Lyndsell was rector of Wickford from 1610 until 1624. He went on to become Bishop of Peterborough in 1632 and Bishop of Hereford in 1634. He is seen here as an effigy on his tomb in Hereford Cathedral.

lord of the manor of Stileman's. The first to exercise this right was Clement Gyselely, who presented Christopher Eton to the living in 1551. However, Queen Mary I's accession to the throne of England in 1553 saw Ralph Byrch installed as rector of Wickford in his place. This may well have been because the Rev. Eton had taken advantage of Henry VIII's decision to allow members of the clergy to marry. When Mary died in 1558, Eton was restored to the living until he resigned of his own accord in 1561.

However, perhaps the Rev. Eton was not a trustworthy incumbent for, by 1565, St Catherine's had reportedly fallen into decay and was in need of repair.

The Rev. Augustine Lyndsell was rector of Wickford from 1610 to 1624. Records from his time describe the rectory as 'a convenient mansion house surrounded by a moat, within which is an old orchard, a garden and dove house; without the moat is a barn and a stable and a hay-house joined together under one roof, an old orchard and about 25 acres of glebe and besides this about 11 or 12 acres of land called

33 St Catherine's Rectory. Although officially led by a rector, the parish of Wickford was often left in the charge of a curate. The rectory building still stands in St Charles Drive.

Lamoland'. Situated on high ground opposite the church on a site now in St Charles Drive, the rectory commanded outstanding views of the surrounding countryside. A square, rather than round, moat such as Wickford rectory possessed was usually constructed for aesthetic purposes rather than being defensive.

Cornelius Gray was presented as rector of Wickford by his patron, Thomas Arnold, in September 1635, by which time the living is recorded as including a great barn called Tyth Barn, a little orchard, a garden plot and 42 acres of glebe. In 1645, however, Gray was taken by Roundhead forces 'for that he hath adhered to the forces raised against parliament and was taken and now continues prisoner'. Parliament put Thomas Lake into the living on

30 August 1645. He was immediately replaced by John Banning, who died in 1646. In that year, the Prayer Book was abolished and the Directory of Public Worship imposed. Gray was reinstated in the parish for a short while but died in 1647.

In 1647, Nicholas Bound became rector by order of the House of Lords, succeeded by Robert Percivall who conformed to the Act of Uniformity by accepting the Book of Common Prayer. In 1660, at the return of Charles II, all sequestered ministers were re-established in their livings and the Commonwealth men expelled.

In 1685, Archdeacon Turner visited Wickford. He found that the rector, Richard Pully, had repaired the chancel and built himself a house.

34 Broadway, looking south, *c.*1900. The *Swan* is on the right, with the grassy patch know as Wickford Green in front.

However, it was noted that the wall under the church steeple and the wooden floor under the pews needed repairing. Also, the stone floor required levelling, the walls needed whitening and the churchyard was full of rubbish.

The Reade Family

The Reade family were well-to-do gentleman farmers, resident at Great Aimes Farm from as early as the late 16th century, and their name is present in various records. For example, in 1594 William Reade, described as 'my well-beloved friend', was made supervisor of the will of David Sympson, the wealthy owner of Linfords in Runwell. Reade was paid 40 shillings for his trouble, at a time when the national average wage was less than one shilling per day. The same William Reade was made an overseer of the will of another friend, the Wickford yeoman Avery Thackwell, in 1595.

The wealth of the family is indicated in court records which show that, on 31 May 1603, Nicholas Garnysh stole seven sheep and a lamb from John Reade. Garnysh was found guilty and was hanged. A similar fate awaited William Heard when he stole a white gelding worth £10 from John Reade, gentleman on 17 December 1608 at Wickford, despite pleading not guilty.

Wickford, Rhode Island, USA

In 1614 a daughter, Elizabeth, was born to Edmund Read of Great Aimes. Elizabeth married John Winthrop jun., the son of the Governor of Massachusetts, in 1635 when he was visiting England. Five days after their marriage Elizabeth and John sailed aboard the *Abigail* to the New World and in 1645 were granted some land, previously occupied by the Narragansett Indians. Elizabeth was so struck by the similarity of the place with her old home that she apparently said, 'Let us call this place Wickford.' Thus came about the name of the town of Wickford in Rhode Island. John Winthrop jun. later became Governor of Connecticut. The couple had five daughters and two sons and the American president, George Bush, is thought to be a descendant of this couple.

When the Rev. Dormer Pierce visited Wickford, Rhode Island in 1907 he commented: 'The land is for the most part untilled, and bears a sad resemblance to the English Wickford in the number of barren acres that the Parish represents.' Dormer Pierce preached in the Rhode Island, Wickford's local church in 1907 on the town's celebration of its hundredth anniversary and he was presented with an engraved silver dish to use in St Catherine's.

Law and Order

The office of Justice of the Peace was instituted in 1361, and the Tudor period saw the expansion of the role of the justices to include the care of the poor and sick, and the maintenance of highways and bridges. During the 16th century, as manors often became financial investments for London businessmen rather than the residences of the nobility, local government began to pass from the lords of the manor and their manorial courts to the parish.

Parishes would elect churchwardens, overseers of the poor, highway surveyors and constables who met quarterly, traditionally in the church vestry, referring problems to the Justices at the Brentwood or Chelmsford Quarter Sessions when necessary.

Not everyone, however, was happy to take on these responsibilities as the Court of Brentwood heard in 1576 when Thomas Geffrey of Wickford 'obstinately refuseth to be churchwarden notwithstanding he was chosen by the parish'. Although this was the most prestigious of the parish offices, perhaps Geffrey

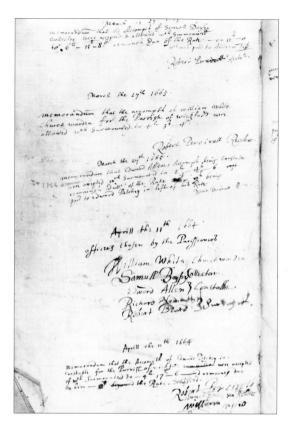

35 Extract from the parish registers, showing the officers chosen by the parishioners in 1664: William White churchwarden, Samuel Bayley collector, Edward Allen constable, and Richard Hammon and Robert Beard surveyors. Also shown are the accounts for 1665, all signed by the rector Robert Percivall.

was uncomfortable in judging his neighbours. For example, in 1620 John Price, a tailor of Wickford, was prosecuted at the instigation of the churchwarden for not going to church for 12 months.

Perhaps the least desirable of the offices was that of highway surveyor, whose duty it was to organise his fellow parishioners in regular road and bridge maintenance. Road mending was a burden to everyone and the Quarter Sessions rolls give long lists of names of those who neglected their duty in this respect. When James Harrys died in 1561, his will included 'To the making and repairing of Wickford Bridge when they shall go about to make it, 5s.'.

36 Wickford Bridge. Everyone travelling from Southend to London had to cross Wickford Bridge.

In 1571 the court heard that 'Burles bridge [Nevendon Bridge] lying in the parish of Wickford is in decay and ought to be made by the inhabitants of the said parish'. In 1572 'Bursbrege' in Wickford is 'clene downe and the parish ought to repair it', and again, in 1574, 'Burres bridge lying within the guildable of Wickford is very noisome and hurtful'. In 1630 the Southend Road and London Road bridges, described as 'one a horse bridge and one a cart bridge', were 'both so decayed that people cannot pass'.

Road repairs often consisted of faggots being cut and bundled up, then placed in holes in the road, covered with stones and gravel, creating soak-aways to help to drain the surface. A court case in 1642 revealed that the inhabitants of Wickford had the right to dig and carry out gravel from 'Chardengate adjoining to Sowlands

in Wickford according to a custom of about 30 years past without payment of a penny or other rent therefore, whereby the highways, for want thereof are extraordinarily decayed'. This gravel pit was on land belonging to Wickford Hall.

Highway surveyors were often frustrated by the lack of co-operation from the parishioners, as demonstrated by the surveyors of Runwell in 1629 who complained at the Quarter Sessions that they had 'laid bushes, stubbed earth and gravel just by the slough and gave them warning to come in with their carts but they would not'. The Midsummer Sessions that year heard that 'two bridges in Wickford … are in great ruin and decay insomuch that in winter time people cannot pass without great danger'.

Maintaining ditches and watercourses was the responsibility of the landowners whose land

37   Nevendon Bridge, *c.*1915. This bridge was replaced in 1935.

38   Swan Lane. Flooding of the streets was a regular occurrence in Wickford. In the 1800s, much of the land in Swan Lane was owned by widow Mrs Bird, remembered in her epitaph as 'the kindest and best of mothers'.

39 Elm Road, named after three tall trees in the road. The cottage seen here at the end of the road was Victoria Cottage; the terraces either side were built by James Gigney *c*.1907.

the water crossed. The river through Wickford was an annoyance in 1597 when it was stated that 'the water hath not his passage'. In 1602, Vincent Simpson (of Beauchamps) and Richard Bundocke (of Wickford Hall) were told they were liable for scouring the river between Wickford and Runwell as neglect caused 'hindrance of the water course … by reason of which the country is greatly annoyed'.

At each Quarter Sessions, the highway surveyors of Wickford presented a list of the people who had not scoured their ditches. For example, in 1667: Robert Percival for 15 rod of ditching in the road between Rawreth Shot and Wickford Church; Edward Allen for 20 rod of ditching in the same road; Sarah Baysey, widow, for 10 rod of ditching in the highway from the church, and Andrew Tyle for not scouring a ditch belonging to the parish houses, he being overseer. In a similar way, in 1693, Robert Barnard a yeoman of Wickford

was indicted for allowing his fences containing one rod in length belonging to his farm next to the highway leading from Rawreth towards Wickford to be in great decay.

The overseers of the poor were responsible for collecting a local rate, which money would be distributed for the relief of the poor as necessary. Parishes were directly responsible for the keep of anyone living in their parish that was unable to support themselves. As well as the unemployed, old or sick, parishioners were responsible for any fatherless children born into their parish. In 1611, William Wolde and John Oudge of Wickford proffered a bill of indictment against Thomas Simonds for 'running away from his dwelling and leaving his child in the parish of Wickford'. In 1651, John Tile the Wickford wheelwright was ordered to appear before the magistrates for having 'begotten Rebecca Theobald with child which bastard child is chargeable to Wickford'.

Similarly, in 1715, Robert Rolf of Downham was called to answer to the inhabitants of Wickford for 'getting Hannah Burrell of that parish with a bastard child, likely to be chargeable to the parish'.

The parish constables were called upon to assist in the collection of local rates, but also to deal with crimes that we would recognise as such today. In 1641, Richard Sable was found guilty of killing Wickford's butcher, John Osbourne, and was imprisoned in Colchester Castle. However, because he could read, Sable was merely branded and released. At the Quarter Sessions held at Chelmsford on 6 March 1651, Thomas Wood a Wickford labourer was indicted for taking the wool of two sheep belonging to Nathaniel Gillman from their bodies, worth 6d. At the same court, the same Thomas Wood was accused of committing incest with his widowed mother Penina Rawlins. Katherine Benison apparently witnessed this.

In 1617, Thomas Carder a husbandman of Wickford stole 25 ewes belonging to widow Priscilla Gudge, each worth six shillings. Carder confessed to the crime and was hanged. When

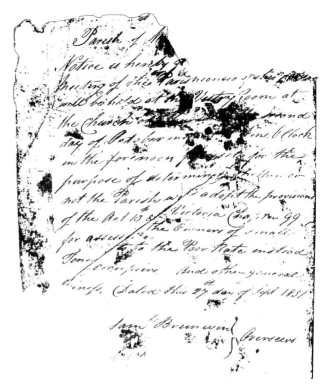

40 Parish notice written by churchwarden Samuel Brunwin in 1851, inviting parishioners to meet to discuss whether the owners rather than the tenants of small properties should pay the Poor Rates.

41 Looking north through the railway bridge. Stileman's can just be seen in the distance.

42 This fire in six of Stileman's haystacks opposite the *Castle* on 11 August 1903 made the local papers. It was thought to have been started by children.

labourer Robert Hopkins was accused of breaking into the house of William Glascocke and stealing a pair of sheets worth 12 shillings he pleaded not guilty and was found not guilty.

Robert Bowen was found guilty of stealing four black heifers each worth 45 shillings belonging to James Shuttlewood, pleaded benefit of the Statutes (he could read from the Bible) and avoided hanging but was branded instead. Also branded was labourer Andrew Tirle who, in 1691, stole three black cows worth £3 each belonging to Anne Snow.

No one, it seems, was safe from the constables' watchful eye, and in 1574 the rector, John Taylor, was presented at the Quarter Sessions for retaining in his service husbandman Nicholas Hemmyng for one half-year, contrary to the statute.

Taxes

Accounts of tax demands help to assess the relative wealth of villages. In 1630, for example, 31 people in Wickford were assessed as wealthy enough to collectively contribute £10 Ship Money for Charles I; 23 Nevendon residents paid £7 and in Pitsea 20 people contributed £11.

An Act of Charles II in 1662 aimed at raising taxes required the local constables to draw up a list of the householders in their parish and the number of fire hearths in each home. These lists were forwarded to the Quarter Sessions and a duplicate copy to the Exchequer. Householders were then required to pay two shillings a year for each hearth in their home. Poor persons who were exempt from parochial rates were also exempt from this tax. That first year, 1662, there were 74 dwellings in Wickford, 20 of which had at least one fire hearth.

In 1671, 21 Wickford residents were assessed for Hearth Tax. The two largest properties stand out: Richard Bundock at Wickford Hall with ten hearths and Allen Roach at Stylemans with nine. There were two other houses in the parish with five hearths each, five houses with four hearths, three houses with three hearths, seven houses with two hearths and two houses with just one fire hearth.

In nearby Runwell, the largest house had only five hearths, in the villages of Nevendon and Basildon the largest number was seven hearths. This indicates the relative wealth of the inhabitants of Wickford at the time.

The Hearth Tax was abolished in 1688.

Four

The Road to Wickford

The 18th century saw an opening up of rural villages like Wickford as road surfaces improved and markets expanded. Although the majority of the local population continued to be engaged in farming, they would have seen greater numbers of travellers through the village and farmers would have found increasing opportunities for marketing surplus produce.

The 1734 list of freeholders indicates only one Wickford resident owning land worth more than £10 – this was Thomas Wright, who owned some land in Hertfordshire. Therefore, all significant landholdings in Wickford were owned by people who were not resident in the parish.

The Land Tax registers of 1781 show Mr Luther as the owner of most land in Wickford, including Wickford Hall and Great Aimes, tenanted respectively by Roger Talbot and Samuel Archer. The only owner-occupiers in the parish at that time were John Matthews and Mark Cook. Land was taxed at four shillings in the pound and the total for Wickford 'with ye guildables' was £94 45s.

Prominent among 18th-century residents was William Ammerson (d.1772), a schoolmaster in Wickford for 12 years; he was also an innkeeper and the parish clerk. The oldest legible gravestones in St Catherine's churchyard

43 London Road, looking west past Ivy Cottage. The main Southend and London roads were characterised by large trees, oaks and elms, abutting the highway.

44   London Road, looking west beyond the bridge.

are in memory of Mary Howlett (d.1733), first wife of Thomas Howlett, the wealthy owner of Bridge House Farm and land at the junction of High Street and London Road, and of her sister, Katherine White (d.1735). However, these headstones were not erected until after Thomas died in 1759, when he left £5 in his will for the purpose, entrusting the job to his friend Chester Moor Hall. Thomas also willed that he be buried between these two ladies, with his own headstone, but there is no evidence of this – perhaps his second wife, Eleanor, had other ideas.

As the village grew, the main population lived along what is now known as the High Street and Broadway; farm labourers would have been accommodated in or near the farmhouse of their employers. There were no buildings on the Southend Road between the bridge and the church, and Bridge House Farm was practically the only building on the London Road.

The main roads were typically wide with green verges along both sides on which livestock could be driven or even pastured; other rights of way were footpaths or narrow cart tracks with high banks and hawthorn thickets. Several farmers preferred the unmade roads of the parish, as it discouraged landlords from visiting their properties, interfering in their management or, perhaps, increasing rents. However, an increase in cart, coach and carriage transport throughout the 18th century was causing considerable damage to the busier roads and locals became annoyed at having to bear the cost of what was effectively 'through traffic'.

An Act of Parliament in 1706, therefore, allowed that certain roads could be gated and tolls charged, thus transferring the cost of the road repairs from the parishes to the road users. Such roads were administered by the Turnpike Trusts, groups of private shareholders.

The Essex Turnpike Trust was granted a turnpike on the road running east from Shenfield, by an Act of Parliament in 1746. The toll road amounted to some 21 miles in length, passing from Shenfield through Billericay and Wickford to Rayleigh where it forked, with one branch continuing to Rochford and the other to Hadleigh and Leigh. Charges to use it ranged from 3d. for a flock of sheep or 2s. 6d. for a carriage. Soldiers, sailors, the clergy, mail coaches and people on their way to church were exempt.

Also in 1746, a petition was presented to Parliament from Wickford, along with North and South Benfleet, Nevendon, Pitsea, Thundersley and Bowers Gifford for turnpiking the road from Wickford to 'the old sea port town' of South Benfleet. This request, however, was rejected, possibly due to opposition from the inhabitants of Leigh who would have lost custom at their port, or perhaps because the north-south routes were primarily used by local traffic. Wickford farmers would transport their corn, calves, sheep, hay and wool to South Benfleet for carriage by sea to London. Returning vessels brought back chalk, which farmers used for conditioning their land. Without the money from a turnpike, however,

trees overgrew the road to the impediment of farm carts, the roads became deeply rutted and sometimes, as Arthur Young recorded in 1767, a team of 20 horses was needed to draw out a succession of chalk wagons stuck fast in the mud. Benfleet eventually achieved a turnpike connection in 1793.

The actual turnpike gate at Wickford is thought to have been on the Southend Road, as records from 1820 refer to this as 'turnpike road'. Although the Wickford tollgate was taken down after a few months, the eastern end of the road continued to collect tolls at Hockley, Rochford and Leigh into the 19th century.

By the end of the 18th century, roads became increasingly devoted to mail and stagecoach services, with restrictions on carrier traffic. A coach service was set up in 1761 to run three times a week from the *Kings Head* at Rochford to Shenfield, passing through Wickford. This service eventually extended through to London

45 Southend Road, at one time known as Turnpike Road. This area of Wickford, being the highest point in the town, was known as The Hills.

46   Looking east across Wickford Bridge to Southend Road, *c.*1930.

with speeds of mail coaches reaching 10 miles per hour (although average speeds were more commonly three miles per hour). Alternatively, villagers could hitch a ride on the Leigh fish cart, which left Leigh at 6p.m. and travelled via Wickford to arrive at Billingsgate market at 4a.m. The ride was dark, bumpy, uncomfortable and smelly … but cheap.

In 1791, mail was sent from London to Brentwood three times a week on Sundays, Wednesdays and Fridays. Letters were collected from there by George Poulton, Rochford's postmaster, whose 18-mile ride from Brentwood to Rochford included Wickford. He received £37 a year for this service, plus a ha'penny for every letter or newspaper he delivered en route and one penny on those he collected. By 1813 this had become a daily service with the route extended to Great Wakering. Riding on horseback, such postmen were often armed with cutlasses and pistols as highwaymen were a real threat. In 1860 John Chapman, driving the Rochford mail coach, was waylaid between Rawreth Shot and Chichester Hall when a

rope was stretched across the road from tree to tree. The impact of the rope on the horse caused the seals of its collar to be broken. A gun was discharged twice but, Philip Benton records, the only victim was 'Her Majesty's mail coach, which was sadly defaced'; John Chapman considered himself lucky to escape alive.

The increase in traffic was not good news for Wickford's bridges and, in 1763, estimates were made for the repair of the Southend Road bridge – poles, planks, piles and irons would cost £34 1d. The bridge was completely rebuilt in 1773. However, only 14 years later the posts and rails had become decayed to such an extent that another £29 worth of repairs was necessary.

Public Houses

The increase in coach traffic through villages in the 18th century, with passengers and horses needing refreshment, were an encouragement to the licensed trade. Inns had begun to flourish in the 14th century, when the lords of manors became increasingly unable or unwilling to

47 An inn known as the *Castle* stood on this site from *c.*1700 to 1998.

accommodate travellers through their estates, and after 1552 all alehouses were required to obtain a licence, becoming subject to official regulations. For example, in 1605, Henry Raye, Richard Weales and Geoffrey Ram were licensed to keep alehouses in Wickford. Thomas Silvester is recorded as an alehousekeeper of Wickford in 1617 when he was tried for felony. In 1631, William Harris was presented by the Runwell constables because he 'selleth beer without a licence and saith he will continue in despite and hath suffered drinking and drunkeness in his house on the Sabbath day'. Court rolls also record a victualler of Wickford named John Herridge in 1701.

Two inns are recorded as trading in Wickford as early as 1714: the *Castle* and the *Kings Head*. The *Castle* was situated in the centre of the village, near Wickford Bridge, and from about 1800 was owned by the Chelmsford brewer

Wells, Hodges and Perry. Its first known licensee was Thomas Emmerson. By 1772 the *Castle* was being run by Richard Kipps, who retained the tenancy until about 1783 when it was taken over by John Lilly. John Lilly ran the pub for over seven years, but by 1800 Robert White had taken over and held the licence for at least another 17 years. In 1836, John Jefferies appealed to the Brentwood magistrates against their decision to refuse him a licence of the *Castle*; his objection was that he had married the previous occupier and merely required a transfer of the licence to his name.

The *Kings Head* was situated on the Southend Road, close to the Rawreth/Wickford parish border, and was let with 15 acres of land, part of the Great Aimes Estate, which included a right of common on Rawreth Shot. During the reign of Queen Anne (1702-14), it was known as the *Queen's Head*. In the 1740s the

48 This photograph, taken *c*.1890, shows the *Swan* inn sign far left. This area of the village, between Wickford Bridge and Swan Lane, was known as Wickford Green. The terrace left of centre is Wickford Place.

inn was tenanted by a Mr Smith for £18 a year. However, Smith let the building get out of repair and 'abused the land' so that the landowner turned him out. The landlord then let the premises to Gabriel Cox at the reduced rent of £14, rather than go to the expense of repairing it.

The next recorded licensee of the *Kings Head* is William Mears in 1769. Mears retained the tenancy until 1785 when Susannah Salmon became the landlady. The inn disappeared from the records after 1788, although the meadow where it was located retained the name 'Kings Head field' into the 19th century. Oak Avenue, opposite Shotgate farmhouse, was built across the site of the *Kings Head*.

Timber

In 1724, the case of Hall Church and Shuttleworth came to court, concerning the cutting of timber on waste land of the Manor of Wickford. The case depended on whether Chester Moor Hall of Stileman's or John Vaughan of Wickford Hall was lord of the manor. The dispute was finally settled in 1731 in favour of Vaughan.

By the end of the 18th century, Wickford's woodland, which at Domesday had comprised over 200 acres, had been reduced to a small copse of 1.2 acres on Great Aimes Farm and

49 The *Swan Inn*, *c*.1890, with landlord Edward Cox standing at the door and an inn sign depicting a large white swan.

50 Looking south from Stileman's. These young ladies are standing just north of the Broadway. On the right of the picture is the garden gate to Stileman's farmhouse; to the left is Stileman's orchard.

one acre on Broomfields Farm, described on the tithe survey as 'bushes'.

The Bell Family

A prominent Wickford family during the 18th century was the Bell family. Holman, writing in the early 18th century, notes a Levi Bell owning land in the town in the 16th century, but the next recorded member of the Bell family in Wickford is Jane, who was buried in St Catherine's in 1705. Levy Bell and Giles Bell held freehold land in Wickford in 1768.

Abraham Bell, tenant of Great Broomfields Farm and a long-serving churchwarden, married his second wife, Ann Milbourn of Great Burstead, in St Catherine's in 1780. One of his two sisters, Mary, married Thomas Wright of Little Bromfords, Wickford (d.1767), while Abraham's son, Thomas, came to own the freehold of Beeches and built the greater part of the house. Thomas had four sons and two daughters, and they continued as prominent members of the community into the 20th century.

The Punt Family

Another family with a long history of residence in Wickford was the Punt family. They first appear in the records in 1770 when Thomas Punt was a ratepayer. In 1775 James Punt was given the tenancy of a farm, following the death of his wealthy father-in-law, yeoman John Heard. James' wife, Mary, was to share the proceeds of her father's estate with her three sisters. However, Mary Punt died before her father, leaving her husband to raise three sons and a daughter alone.

James Punt appears again in the will of Martha Hall in 1782 where he is noted as the tenant of Stileman's, and for the following 50 years members of the Punt family are listed as Wickford ratepayers. When the Punts appear in 19th-century records, however, they are no longer tenant farmers but mere agricultural labourers, on occasion having to resort to parish relief.

The Poor and the Sick

Although the 18th century was a time of progress for the landowning classes, for the

51   Stileman's and Wickford Place. This row of terraced cottages, known as Wickford Place, was pulled down in the 1960s and replaced with a row of shops.

agricultural labourers life continued to be ruled by the harvests. In poor growing seasons, or in times of ill-health, they were entirely dependent on the generosity of their neighbours. Before 1834, the parish overseers were responsible for the care of the poor and the sick; they collected a rate from the parishioners for distribution to the needy and could buy or rent property for housing the poor. In 1796, the Wickford overseers distributed £200 to the villagers but in 1800 the bill came to £445 as it had been a year of particularly bad harvests.

In 1759, the Wickford parish overseers were renting a property from John Glascock for 30 shillings a year in which to house the poor. Fifty years later they had a similar arrangement with Thomas Bell, in 1815 paying him a half yearly rent of £4 4s. They also paid the rent for those who could not pay their own, for example, paying Thomas Bell £2 rent for Blakley's house and £2 12s. 6d. for Lilly's.

In 1816, the parish paid £1 2s. 6d. for 500 bricks for the poor house, £3 3s. 6d. for a

bedstead for the poor house and coal for the poor at 1s. 6d. per bushel. Poor men would receive between 7s. and 16s. per week to support themselves and their families, while other individuals listed in the overseers' accounts, such as the 'fouer widers at ye porehouse', each received 2s. per week. However, such charity was not always graciously given and it appears to have been with some pique that John Heard, then overseer, wrote in large letters in his accounts:

> Joseph French has cost the parish of Wickford since the yeare 1763 to the yeare 1780 exclusive of cloathes and all other caselties one hundred and forty three pounds three shillings.

Orphans and children whose parents could not afford to keep them were sometimes boarded out at the expense of the parish. For example, the overseers recorded in 1756:

> William Purkis takes John Ingold at 1s. 6d. per week until he arrive at the age of 12 years and then but 1s. until he arrive at the age of 16 to be paid by the overseers and then the said William Purkis is

52 Runwell Road, looking north. The field on the left became the village cricket field. It was enclosed by 64 grand elm trees, but these were all lost to Dutch Elm Disease in the early 1950s.

to double cloath him out and not discharge him before on forfeit of five pounds to the overseers of the parish.

In 1816 Dame Sarah Thurogood was receiving £1 4s. per week for housing Susannah Woolard, who had been with her since 1813, Eleanor, Phoebe, William and Jane Glassocks, and the three Witamores: Julia, Eliza and Elizabeth. By 1818, Sarah Thurogood was boarding nine children for which she received £1 12s. per week. The good lady was dependent upon this income for, between 1785 and 1802, she had lost four baby sons of her own, all less than 15 months old, while her husband Thomas died aged 52 in 1808.

As soon as they were old enough, children were found suitable employment. For example, in 1757, Edward Fairhead agreed with the parish 'to learn William Waylett to mende shoes and bootes in workmanlike manner'. Thomas Hone was bound apprentice to Benjamin Hall of Chelmsford in April 1818, for which the Wickford overseers paid £38. Girls would usually be found a domestic situation. Occasionally, it was not just the children who needed housing and, in 1817, Mr White received two shillings for lodging the whole Punt family.

In addition, payments could be made for specific purchases, such as: '1 pair of stockings for Joseph Watts 2s. 6d.', 'Cotton shirt for John

Blakeley 6s.'. On 2 December 1815, Dame Swan was allowed nine shillings to 'buy some coals with' and, in March 1817, the overseers recorded 'Mrs Scott to buy her child some clothes £1', while the shoemakers sent their bills direct to overseers: 'Mr Moyes shoes for the poor £9 11s. 6d.'.

Occasionally, it was impossible to find long-term accommodation for a family within Wickford. This was the case with John Beach, his wife and three children, who were taken to Stock and lodged in the workhouse there.

With poverty and poor housing conditions, infant mortality was high and death was no stranger to the village. The notebook of Sarah Thurogood provides insight into the dangers the population faced:

> Thomas Chambers died February 22nd 1823 aged 11 months. Thomas William Chambers died August 18th 1828. Both died from whooping

cough ... Smallpox was inoculated at Wickford May 3rd 1818. 111 were inoculated by the parish. James Carter deceased ... Sarah Chambers died December 1st 1817 aged 30 years. Baby born dead November 11th.

However, the community took care of the dying and would pay for someone to maintain a 24-hour vigil. For example 'Edward Hymas for setting up two nights with John Turner 4s.'. This service had its perks: 'William White for gin and beer for the people who set up with J. Marshal 7s. 9½d.'.

If the worst happened, the parish also paid for funeral expenses:

> December 28th 1815 paid Mr Sneezman for a coffin and shroud for Lark £1 4s. 6d. Two women for laying out Lark 3s. Six men for carrying Lark up to church 9s. Paid the minersters and clarks fees 5s. 6d.

The parish, however, was sometimes able to reclaim some of their expenses from the sale

53 Chapel Row, Runwell Road. This terrace stood just south of the Congregational cemetery. In 1899 all six cottages sold for £375. They were demolished after being damaged by a landmine falling in the cricket field opposite on 2 October 1940.

54 Nevendon Road, 1913. About this time the Peculiar People religious sect built a corrugated iron chapel near here, now a permanent building and part of the Union of Evangelical Churches.

of the deceased's property: 'received by Lilly's goods £8 19s. 10d.'.

Strangers would also be dealt with charitably: 'Paid Joseph Wright for setting up with the man who broke his leg 3 nights 6s.', and 'relieved a man and woman in distress 6d.', 'relieved four men with a pass from Harwich 4s.'. These last would have been sailors dependent on the generosity of the villages they passed through as they travelled home on leave from their ship.

Poverty, of course, often led to crime. However, whether someone was reported to the Quarter Session Courts was often left to the churchwarden's discretion. Wickford's stocks stood adjacent to the churchyard and, no doubt, petty criminals served their punishment there. The churchwarden occasionally benefited; for example, in 1814 the churchwarden's accounts include: 'received of Sheepard on account of his being convicted of steeling cabbages from Robert Smith 10s.'.

At Christmas 1786, the churchwarden had to pay five shillings 'for mening the church windows whant dammag by theves', and the following April paid five shillings 'for mending the church huch when brock oppen'. The hutch was the box or chest that held the registers and sometimes the church plate.

Other expenses the overseers of the poor incurred included: 'June 1823 Journey to attend at Brentwood for the purpose of taking out orders of filiation on James Mascall, the reputed father of Eliza Whitmore's child £2 6d.'. No doubt this was the same poor Eliza 'Witamore' who with her sisters had been taken in by Sarah Thurogood in 1816.

Calling a doctor was an expensive undertaking, particularly if no medic was resident in the parish. It was the overseers' and churchwardens' responsibility to secure medical services for the poor of the parish, and in 1812 Dr B. Daranda signed the following statement in the churchwardens' accounts:

55 Nevendon Road, 1935. The same view as the previous picture, 22 years later.

I hereby agree to attend the poor of Wickford both in surgery physic and midwifery, fractures, journeys and smallpox for the yearly sum of six guineas – journeys out of the parish to be paid at the rate of one shilling a mile beyond the parish – this agreement is made for three years ensuing. It is understood that all midwifery cases with illegitimate children are to be paid for, one guinea each, if attendance is required.

In 1834, a new Poor Law Act sought to simplify and centralise the administration of the poor and, to this end, parishes were grouped into 'Unions', the main town of which would provide a workhouse for those unable to support themselves, including the poor, sick or children. Wickford became part of the Billericay Union and its poor were sent to the Union Workhouse built in 1840 on the site of the present St Andrew's Hospital. The workhouse was described by White's *Directory* as 'a large and commodious building with room for 270 paupers'.

By the end of the 18th century, a working man's wage could be as much as 13 shillings a week, although farm labourers were earning nearer nine shillings, with boys earning two shillings. Rising food prices meant that, without poor relief, many large families would have been close to starvation on this wage.

The Parish Boundary

Entitlement to poor relief and the exact amount of that relief was dependent upon the parish in which one lived. The 1662 Act of Settlement restricted the movement of people who were not freeholders, lest they become a burden on the poor relief of another parish. Similarly, the taxes that landowners paid depended upon in which parish their land lay. Thus parish boundaries were of much importance. The 'beating of the bounds' of the parish was an annual event whereby the rector and several important villagers and landholders, together more often than not with a crowd of boisterous children, would walk around the limits of the parish, marking significant points as indicators of the bounds (for example by scoring a cross on large trees).

The festive occasion was a cause for celebration and usually included a meal paid for from the churchwardens' rates. In 1776, for example, churchwarden Abraham Bell noted in his accounts 'paid half the expence that was spent in going the bouns of the parish'. In May 1806 parishioners enjoyed dinner at the *Castle Inn* after having accompanied the rector of Hanningfield on a tour of 'the boundary of that part of Wickford parish lying east from Wickford Castle …'. In May 1824, the churchwarden paid £4 14s. 'for dinner at the sign of the Castle when the parishioners went the bounds of the parish'. The full cost of the meal was £9 8s., half the cost being paid by the rector, the Rev. Peter Whish.

By 1800, the Land Tax for Wickford was £99 4s., with the guildables listed separately: £26 8s. for the eight parcels of land in Rawreth guildable and £8 for the 12 plots in Runwell guildable. Francis Fane (Wickford Hall) and William Cockerton (Stileman's) had replaced Mr Luther as the main landowners.

Five

A Victorian Village

Rural Essex was hit by an agricultural depression in 1815, which continued for some 20-30 years during which tenant farmers, as well as their labourers, saw their incomes fall. In 1832 Wickford was a close-knit community with a population of 402, and Pigott's *Directory* reported: 'There is nothing worthy of note attached to this place either as regards trade or curiosity.' However, when Queen Victoria succeeded to the throne in 1837, Wickford, along with the rest of Britain, embarked on a period of innovation and change, leading White's *Directory* of 1848 to describe Wickford as 'compact and well-built'.

The population increased steadily throughout the 19th century, apart from a noticeable drop in population during the 1850s, the consequence of a serious outbreak of cholera in 1854.

The lord of the manor for the first half of the century was Colonel John Fane who owned Wickford Hall, Great Aimes and The Wick. Like his predecessors, Colonel Fane was not resident in the parish and, therefore, Wickford Hall remained nothing more than a large farmhouse, rather than developing into a prestigious manorial residence. Despite this, tenants were bound by strict conditions of tenure and landowners held ultimate power in the parish.

56 The Upson family took over Reed's blacksmith's shop at Foundry Corner (now Hall's Corner) and ran a saddler's business. This photograph was taken *c.*1910. The photographer is standing in Nevendon Road.

57 London Road, looking east.

John Fane's accounts of his Wickford property indicate the particular value of timber and are shown in the table below. For the tenant farmers, however, it was wheat that was providing the major source of income. During the Napoleonic wars, much land had been laid to corn as imports reduced and swathes of land stood yellow with ripening corn, protected by Corn Laws (1815-44). In all, 1,740 acres of Wickford was under cultivation.

William Cockerton, also an absentee landlord, was the second largest landholder in the area. He inherited considerable property in Wickford from his cousin, Martha Hall of Brentwood, and owned Stileman's Farm until his death in 1858.

John Brewitt (Bridge House), Samuel Brunwin (Stileman's) and Thomas Bell (Beeches), all landholders, together with the men who tenanted the other farms, took on the roles of those with the highest social status in the village. They became the parish overseers and churchwardens, responsible for the day-to-day running of the parish, administering affairs via the traditional vestry meetings. The control of the village lay in their ability to dismiss their employees and, through the parish offices they held, grant or refuse poor relief. They also constituted the most affluent, and therefore most important, customers to the village artisans and tradespeople.

Agriculture continued as the main employment in the parish, with the farm labourers' average wage being 1s. 7d. a day or 9s. 6d. per week. Low wages were common in Wickford where employers were small tenant farmers,

May 1st 1828	A journey to Wickford to measure timber	10s
	Gave the timber fallers	5s
September 28th 1828	A letter from Wickford about timber	8d
October 1829	Received of Mr Archer for timber	20-4-3
	Received of Mr Offen for timber	361-10-0
	Received of Mr Patmore for timber	40-16-0

already burdened with increasing taxes and parish rates. Increased mechanisation also encouraged low wages and unemployment.

Wickford soil was considered to be rich and loamy and, along with the main wheat crop, oats were grown, as well as beans, peas, barley for the London breweries and turnips for cattle fodder. Land was managed and cultivated 'according to the custom of the neighbourhood' using the five-course shift system of husbandry, whereby one fifth of the arable land stood fallow each year (although some farms worked on a six-course system). Cottagers kept their own chickens, or sometimes a pig, and grew vegetables to supplement their meagre incomes.

From 1800, labourers were more likely to be accommodated in rented or 'tied' cottages, rather than board with the farmer's family. The 'tied' dwellings were reserved for the agricultural workers of a particular farm – if you lost your job, you also lost your home. Cottages were small and, with no local building stone, the oldest homes were built of wattle and daub with thatched roofs. Later, traditional Essex weather-boarded cottages were the norm. Several homes had freshwater wells, while others were dependent on surface streams or public wells, and for most the toilet was a privy at the bottom of the garden.

Overcrowding of these cottages was within the remit of the Billericay Sanitary Inspectors and landlords were threatened with summonses for allowing overcrowded conditions. In the early 1880s, Samuel Brunwin was ordered to remedy the overcrowding in both Adey's and Nash's cottage, and proceedings were taken to stop overcrowding at Elsdon's and Letch's. Mr Keys was called upon to give up his lodger or have his cottage closed for overcrowding.

Life would have been hard for the agricultural labourers, working 6a.m. to 6p.m. in summer and every hour of daylight in winter, six days a week. Even children were set to work picking stones and scaring crows off growing crops and assisting with the harvest.

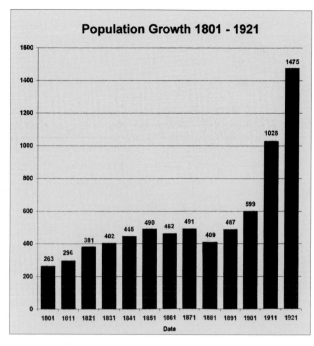

58 Population growth chart. The population of Wickford steadily increased during the 1800s, apart from a slight fall due to a severe outbreak of cholera in 1854, and a larger decline during the 1870s' agricultural depression when many people moved away.

Typically of rural villages at that time, poaching was prevalent in Wickford. For example, in 1792, John Jarvis, a barber, was fined 20s. (reduced to 10s.) for 'sporting without a certificate', and William Purkis, a butcher, was fined 20s. for the same offence.

Country folklore prevailed and the ghost of a black dog was said to wander in the Congregational Chapel burial ground in Runwell Road, while a cottage on the corner of Southend Road and Wick Lane was said to be haunted by the ghost of a poor old woman who had been refused food at the nearby rectory.

A Journey through Wickford

Travellers from London to Rayleigh in the early 19th century would pass Bridge House Farm on the deeply rutted London Road, wet and slimy in winter, baked hard in the summer.

59   Graylin's grocer's shop, south-east side of the High Street.

They would hear the hammer on anvil as they turned the corner into the High Street at Thomas Reed's foundry and smithy with its three forges, wood smoke pervading the air. This street was the centre of the parish, where most of the village's buildings and particularly its tradespeople were concentrated, between Foundry Corner (now Hall's Corner) and Stileman's farmhouse. Without the railway bridge, of course, the Broadway did not exist as a separate road.

Continuing up the road, travellers would pass the public water pump on their left, the focus of much activity in the village as the main source of water for many. Water was collected in buckets by women and children, typically using two buckets swinging from a yoke carried across the shoulders.

Despite its location on the Crouch and regular flooding of the streets, the supply of fresh water was a constant concern in Wickford. As the population grew, the traditional sources, surface streams, springs and private wells, were unable to cope with demand and, in 1835, the parish acquired a small plot of land to combat the problem. Here, where Market Road joins the High Street today, a deep well was dug, with a public pump set up over it. The Billericay Union Rural Sanitary Authority inspectors were charged with repairing the water pump at Wickford anytime it was out of repair. However, less than fifty years after the pump was installed, demand for water was again beginning to outstrip supply and, as discussed later, the village pump caused much heated debate in the village.

A second focus of activity in the main street was the *Castle Inn*, owned by Chelmsford brewers Wells and Perry and often used to conduct public business or sales of property, in the absence of any other meeting rooms. The Billericay Foxhounds met two or three times a year at the *Castle* before making their way to Colonel Kemble's wood, now the site of Runwell Hospital, for their hunt.

The *Castle Inn* also served as a coach stop and in 1836 there was one coach a day from *The Bull* at Aldgate to Southend, travelling via Ilford, Romford, Brentwood, Billericay, Wickford, Rayleigh and Rochford. This was the *Despatch* owned by James Tabor & Co. It left Southend at 7.45a.m. to reach London at 1.45p.m., returning at 2.45p.m. to reach Southend at 8.45p.m. Four people were carried inside and 11 outside the coach. In addition, a Rochford coach, owned by J. Thurogood, passed through Wickford on Monday to Saturday, on its way to the *Blue Boar* in Aldgate.

From the 1840s Thomas and William Pease operated a passenger coach service from Wickford's *Castle Inn*. After the railway reached Brentwood in 1840, a coach from Rochford to Brentwood railway station passed through Wickford at 8.40a.m. on Mondays, Wednesdays, Fridays and Saturdays, returning in the early evening.

Moses Murray ran a regular coach service to Chelmsford on Fridays from about 1860 to 1902 and, in the 1870s-80s, Collard Thomas operated a service from Nevendon to Chelmsford which passed through Wickford every Friday. Edward Cox, the second licensee of the *Swan*, ran a service to Chelmsford on Tuesdays and Fridays

60 The *Castle Hotel* (formerly *Inn*). Note the steam train on the railway bridge.

61   The *Swan Inn*. Members of the Patmore family were licensees here for 57 years.

from the 1880s until the early 20th century, when Charles Cox took over until 1912.

Just beyond the *Castle Inn*, the main road turned east across Wickford Bridge. North of the bridge on the west side of the road, the *Swan Inn* opened in a double-fronted house on the corner of Swan Lane in about 1880. The first licensee was an injured war veteran. Beyond the *Swan* was Stileman's farmhouse and, opposite it, an orchard and the 'drinkings' where villagers would take their horses and cattle to quench their thirst in the River Crouch. They shared this stretch of river with kingfishers diving for sticklebacks and village boys doing the same. The river also served as the village's main sewer, privies being built over open ditches that drained into the Crouch.

Wickford Bridge was often impassable to pedestrians, being regularly flooded, while the incline of the Southend Road beyond it would be deeply rutted and muddy. Elm trees lined the road and often overhung it, leaving the road in pitch darkness on a winter evening, perhaps just the dim light of a tallow-dipped candle or rushlight visible in a cottage window. Even into the 20th century, local residents recalled that visitors only came on nights when the moon was full; at other times it was too dark to find one's way home again. During summer, beyond the tree line, pasture and arable land stretched as far as the eye could see.

South of the Southend Road was Beeches farmhouse, and on the crest of the hill clustered Wickford Hall Farm, Wickford Hall, St Catherine's church and the rectory.

Wickford Hall

Wickford Hall was built at the highest point in the parish. By the 1850s, it had four large reception rooms, six bedrooms, a bathroom, three WCs, a garage, stabling and 'extensive and charming old-world gardens', extending to over three acres. The house was principally brick built and roughcast with a tiled roof, having been 'converted from the old manor house'. Its southern aspect was approached by a pretty carriage drive with clipped gold yew hedging. The oak entrance porch led into a hall and

62   Mayes ironmongery and hardware shop, far left, operated from premises on the corner of Station Approach from 1910 to 1960.

then to a 32ft by 17ft 6in dining room with French casements to the garden; the room had a tiled open fireplace with decorated mantle, and wood-block flooring. The drawing room was 20 by 15ft plus a small bay window, and a well-grate in a tiled hearth with enamelled mahogany mantel. There was also a breakfast room of 19ft 6in by 15ft with an open fire, and a study of 20 by 14ft 3in with another fireplace. The kitchen, with its Eagle range and sink, was complemented by a back lobby, larder, scullery with stove and sink, a tiled dairy and a WC.

Upstairs, the four main bedrooms measured 20 by 15ft, 15 by 14ft, 20 by 14ft and 17 by 13ft in size. The fifth bedroom was fitted with linen cupboards, while the sixth had access to a secondary staircase from the kitchen. By the early 20th century, the bathroom had a porcelain enamel bath, heated towel airer, hot and cold water and a WC.

Adjoining the house was a garage and coach house, loosebox and stall, harness room with a loft over, and a tool room. There was also a washhouse, boothouse, acetylene gas store, wood and coal shed and workshop.

The gardens comprised flowering and evergreen shrubs and trees, herbaceous plants, roses, bulbs and included a tennis lawn. The separate kitchen garden boasted fruit trees and bushes including upwards of 500 blackcurrant bushes, a vinery and tomato house. The orchard was well-stocked with 300 young standard and pyramid fruit trees 'of the most select varieties', and this is where a timber and felt semi-intensive 61 ft by 12ft 6in poultry house with a concrete floor stood.

A report on Wickford Hall Farm in 1828 records that the land was of a 'sound, rich nature, well calculated for yielding abundant crops in the six course system of husbandry'. This method of crop rotation followed the pattern: fallow and coleseed or turnips, barley and oats, clover, wheat, beans and finally wheat or fallow. The farmhouse was 'substantially built of cement blocks' with a tiled roof and approached from Highcliff Road and included a large parlour, living room, scullery, and three

63 Gigney's shop, Broadway, *c.*1900. James Gigney started in Wickford as a saddler in 1837. His son, James Gigney jun. expanded into drapery, ironmongery and grocery.

bedrooms. The earth closet was outside with the coalhouse, tool house and poultry house. Extensive farm buildings included a pair of brick-built cottages, each with a parlour, kitchen, scullery and two bedrooms.

St Catherine's church and churchyard stood adjacent to Wickford Hall.

A New Church

Local historian William Henry King visited St Catherine's church in September 1851 but was not impressed. It 'retains little of its ancient character having been coarsely patched and repaired from time to time ... and is now in a very dilapidated condition', he wrote. He noted that a former rector, the Rev. Peter Beauvoir (1761-1822), had died in possession of a fortune of well over one million pounds but was evidently 'not piously inclined to spend a shilling of it upon the house of God'.

However, the 'ponderous oak panelled ceiling' was admired. Twenty years later King found the church in 'much the same disgraceful and dilapidated condition' and noted that the inside was 'crammed with puritanical boxes miscalled pues'.

The parishioners apparently agreed with Mr King's opinions and a meeting held in the vestry on 22 October 1874 resolved that it was 'expedient to rebuild the parish church of Wickford', as it was both dilapidated and unable to accommodate the growing population of the town.

A list of subscribers was immediately drawn up, headed by the main contributor, the Rev. W. Hugo Lukin, who gave £400 raised from a mortgage on the rector's stipend. The other main contributors were farmers David Archer, Thomas Bell and Henry Stone who gave £50 each, while saddler James Gigney donated £25.

64 St Catherine's church, *c*.1905. This building dates from 1876. The gate on the right leads to Wickford Hall.

65 Wickford's second Congregational Chapel, built in 1897 in the High Street, is seen here *c*.1908. The gate beside the chapel led to the Great Eastern Railway reservoir.

Colonel John Fane, the main landholder in the parish at the time, generously donated £7, while the list of subscribers included 'Little Rosie' and 'Little Mable' who gave 10s. 6d. (half a guinea) each. Proceeds from concerts amounted to £21 11s., while a bazaar raised £114 9s. 8d.

The last service held in the 14th-century St Catherine's church was on 30 May 1875. The building was then demolished and the replacement church was built of stone in the Early English style, retaining certain features of its predecessor including the oak roof from Prittlewell Priory, with a chancel, nave, vestries, south porch and a turret at the west end containing two bells. The total subscriptions raised, £1,778 1s. 8d., not only paid for the main fabric of the church building itself but also a complete re-fit inside; for example, a new pulpit for £18 18s. and 300 hassocks for £1 11s. 6d. The new church was consecrated by the Bishop of Rochester, the Rt. Rev. Thomas Claughton, on 9 November 1876.

Two stained glass windows commemorate Henry Stone, a former churchwarden who died in 1883, another window is dedicated to Henry Aubrey Bell who died in Rio de Janeiro in 1877, while a third window is for Dr John Marshall who served the parish for 48 years.

There was a pound near the churchyard where livestock were temporarily kept, and Mr Sneezum was paid £2 10s. 6d. out of the churchwardens' rates for making and erecting new village stocks, in addition to the £1 12s. 8d. paid to William Reed for 'blacksmith's work to new stocks'.

The rectory opposite the church commanded magnificent views of the surrounding countryside. Left in the care of curates, the building remained unchanged for decades until extended by the Rev. Hugo Lukin in 1867 and given a new front by the Rev. George Porter in 1897. In hard winters during the

Rev. George Porter's incumbency (1888-98) the rectory moat, then surrounding three sides of an old orchard, became the site of skating parties for the parishioners; on dark evenings, if there was no moon, people would bring their carriage lamps and fix them to shine on the ice. Hard winters were probably not such fun for the labourers who had to go about their business on roads and fields where snow was as high as the hedges.

Congregationalism

While the Rev. John Thornton was minister of Billericay's Congregational Church he was inspired to extend his ministry to the neighbouring villages. He was no doubt encouraged by Wickford parishioners, disheartened by their difficult journey to St Catherine's across the regularly flooded Wickford Bridge and by a rector who spent little time in the parish. Thus, the Rev. Thornton brought about the building of Wickford's first Congregational Chapel in Runwell Road in 1811. The inauspicious site on the flood plain at the extremity of the parish would have meant that the land was cheap, an important consideration for the independents or 'dissenters' who, until 1868, were obliged to pay church rates in addition to funding their own buildings. Mary Manning Hardy bequeathed £10 p.a. to the chapel, while another £28 p.a. accrued from donations from Mr Richardson and Samuel Brunwin.

The chapel's popularity under the leadership of its own minister, the Rev. J. Smith, resulted in an extension in 1816, almost doubling the size of the building. However, in 1870, led by the new minister George Garlick, the Congregationalists decided that the condition of the building had deteriorated to an unacceptable extent.

The 'seatholders', as regular members of the congregation were called, consulted an architect whose verdict was that it was 'most undesirable, if not impossible, to make anything of the

66 Interior of Congregational Chapel, *c*.1920. The chapel was pulled down in 1972 for town centre redevelopment.

old building'. He corroborated this view by describing the old chapel as 'badly designed, badly situated, and badly built'.

The congregation agreed that during the regular flooding of the Crouch it was impossible to reach the chapel at all. The walls were rent by settlements, the roof was rotten and leaking, the floor, doors and windows were defective, while the gallery and pews were 'most inconvenient in arrangement and ugly in construction'.

Therefore, the congregation purchased for £70 from James Bartlett a plot of land on the east side of the High Street and work began in February 1875 on a new building of 42ft by 28ft 6in, to accommodate 90 people plus an additional 50 people in the gallery. A memorial stone was incorporated into the building in April 1875, laid with a silver trowel and mallet by George Brunwin. The finished

construction of red brick relieved with white bricks and Bath stone was described by the Rev. George Garlick as 'Romanesque' and 'elegant'. Garlick himself was credited with having rebuilt the church from nothing 'both materially and spiritually' during his ministry at Wickford from 1870 to 1882. However, his personal life was not so happy at this time: between 1874 and 1878, five of his own children died, all under the age of eight.

In 1891, a schoolroom, also used as the village reading rooms, was added to the chapel, and a manse was provided on land donated by two members of the congregation. At this time there were about 74 regular worshippers. Notable pastors include A.C. Potter who was invited to lead the church in 1903 at a salary of £100 p.a. He remained in the village for 40 years with his wife who served as organist. The original cemetery in Runwell Road continued in use.

67 A Church of England school was built on this site on Southend Road in 1861, with much of the building costs being met by public subscription. The original school was thatched and was totally destroyed by fire in January 1908. The current building dates from November 1908.

The chapel was demolished in 1972 to make way for town centre redevelopment.

Education

In 1807, William Potter, curate of Downham and Wickford, confirmed to the Bishop of London that education in Wickford consisted of a Sunday school of about 25 pupils and a day school of 23, both taught by the same person.

However, by 1841 there was at least one private school in the village and the 1851 census indicates three 'Dame schools', run by three married ladies, Eleanor Crow, Eliza Flack and Mary Champion, and catering for up to 70 scholars between them. The more wealthy residents may have employed a governess, as did the Rev. Lukin, or even, as Thomas Bell did, sent children to boarding school.

A rising population and a perceived need to educate the children of the poor led the Church of England to instigate the building of a National School in 1861, on land belonging to John Fane in the furthest corner of the Wickford Hall Estate. The school was designed by Mr Moss and built by carpenter John Carter and bricklayer George Carter. Funds to build the school were raised by public subscription, although the main contributors were members of the clergy, the Reverends Berens, De Tessier, Purvis and Lukin and their friends. Farmers David Archer and Thomas Bell gave £20 each, newly widowed Mrs Brewitt of Bridge House Farm gave £15 and Henry Stone, the new tenant of Wick Farm, gave £7 2s., total contributions amounting to £288 14s. 11d.

The resulting school, a single-storey thatched building with an attached house for a master, was large enough for 75 pupils, and Mrs Eliza Flack, who had previously run her own school in the High Street, was appointed as the first teacher.

In 1870, education became compulsory and villages were empowered to create School

68 The Church of England School. Throughout the 19th century pea-picking, blackberrying, harvests and outbreaks of disease caused much absenteeism.

69 Runwell School, *c.*1900. This school was built by Runwell's rector the Rev. Beresford Harris, and lord of the manor Thomas Kemble. The school closed in 1914; its porch was removed and the children had to attend Wickford School.

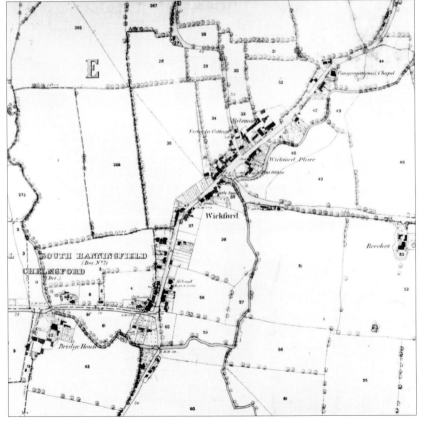

70 Broadway shops, *c.*1900. George English's grocery, far right, served as Wickford's post office for many years.

71 Extract from 1st edition OS map, 1898. Buildings were sparse in Wickford at this time; most were in the High Street.

Boards and levy education rates. About this time, the Runwell church school closed down and children from Runwell joined those from Nevendon along roads that were flooded nearly every winter to attend Wickford School.

The 1873 Agricultural Children's Act outlawed the employment of children under eight in agriculture, but school attendance still suffered at harvest times. Boys in particular would help with potato picking, plough driving, rook scaring and stone picking. In 1886, when Mrs Catherine Douglas was mistress, only 50 pupils attended on average, despite which an additional classroom was added to the school in 1894.

Postal Services

In 1832, Wickford became a post town. Letters were received from Ingatestone via mailcart and distributed by sub-postmaster Moses Miller who despatched outgoing letters via Billericay at 6.45p.m.

When Ingatestone railway station opening in 1845, mail for south-east Essex was carried by train as far as Ingatestone, and was then transferred to a mail coach which travelled to Southend via Billericay, Wickford, Rayleigh and Rochford.

Enclosure of Rawreth Shot Common

Throughout the 19th century, many villages saw common land enclosed and divided between private landowners or tenants, landowners feeling that even a small rental income was preferable to none. In 1855, Thomas Bell was charged with the valuation and division of the land comprising Rawreth Shot and drew up plans for its division, which were

subsequently approved by the magistrates. Most of the Wickford section of the common came into the ownership of John Fane; two small plots of just over one acre were awarded to David Archer, and one acre of land, then in Rawreth but now part of Wickford, came to Daniel Brown Grout. At this time Great Aimes became known as Shot Farm. Within a few years, the whole aspect of the common changed – gardens and vegetable plots taking the place of scrub and coarse grazing.

The End of an Era

In 1870, John Going's *Gazetteer of England and Wales* described Wickford thus:

> Wickford, a village, a parish and a sub-district, in Billericay district, Essex. The village stands on the River Crouch, 4 miles N by E of Pitsea railway station; is an ancient place, and has a post office under Chelmsford. The parish comprises 1,758 acres. Real property, £3,426. Pop 462. Houses 105. The property is divided among a few. Wickford Hall is a farmhouse. The living is a rectory in the diocese of Rochester. Value £939. Patron R.B. Berens, Esq. The church is old but good and there is an Independent chapel.

The second agricultural depression of the century in the 1880s affected the whole village. While the loss to agricultural workers was direct, the shopkeepers and craftsmen also felt the loss of trade. Blacksmiths, too, found themselves in competition with specialist manufacturers.

By the end of Queen Victoria's reign in 1901, Wickford boasted a population of 600 persons. Its residents benefited from regular postal and coach passenger services and the rural trades were diversifying. The Hundred as a unit of administration had practically disappeared, replaced by Sanitary Districts, Poor Law Unions and District Councils.

Six

Meet the Neighbours 1840-1870

In 1831, only eight out of Wickford's population of 402 were landowners and entitled to vote in parliamentary elections. These were David Archer, Thomas Bell, Samuel Brunwin, Jacob Cranfield of Quakers farm, Joseph Crow, James Byass, William Whitfield and James Larrett. At the opposite end of the social scale, 57 men were employed as agricultural labourers, typically among the poorest workers in England. After agricultural labourers, the most common profession in the village was carpenter, there being four or five in Wickford at any one time, closely followed by shoemakers. Blacksmiths, wheelwrights, saddlers and harnessmakers, who co-operated to keep horses and carts, the vital tools of agriculture, in good working order, were also well represented in Wickford. There were at least two blacksmiths and two wheelwrights in Wickford at any one time throughout the 19th century. Agriculture also provided a large proportion of the income of carpenters, builders and painters. Therefore, when agriculture was doing well, the whole village prospered, including the tradesmen who depended on the custom of their agricultural neighbours.

Despite 18th-century road improvements, and 'outsiders' coming into the village to work or marry, Wickford remained a remote, close-knit rural parish where people spoke the local country dialect, often incomprehensible to non-locals, and country folklore prevailed.

By 1841 the population of the village was 445, rising to 490 in 1851. Although less than half the population (205) were born in the town itself, most were born locally, e.g. Downham (16), Runwell (14), Ramsden Bellhouse (12), and very few hailed from outside Essex.

John Brewitt of Bridge House Farm was perhaps the wealthiest of Wickford's farmers, managing some 1,300 acres in Wickford and neighbouring parishes and employing 70 agricultural labourers as well as three house servants. He too contributed to parish life, serving as both churchwarden and overseer of the poor. He died in 1860 and was buried in his family vault in Downham churchyard, leaving the farm in the charge of his widow Maria. Their daughters Hester and Elizabeth were wealthy enough to be land proprietors in their own right, while Maria continued to employ a cook, a housemaid and a coachman.

Another wealthy Wickford resident was Samuel Brunwin (b.1798) who lived as a tenant of Stileman's Farm with his wife Susan and children George and Mary Ann. Their household in 1841 included Levi Bartlett, employed as an agricultural labourer, and two young house servants. Susan Brunwin, in common with the other farmers' wives, would have overseen the running of the household and been involved with the dairying and feeding the farmyard poultry, although the dirtiest jobs would have been left to the servants. In 1858, following the death of landowner William Cockerton, Samuel Brunwin bought Stileman's outright. Widowed ten years earlier, he lived with his daughter, Mary Ann, and younger son, Thomas,

72   The south end of High Street, looking north, *c.*1920. Mr Fairhead took over Graylin's grocery store.

and was wealthy enough to employ three live-in house servants as well as six men and three boys on his farm. In addition, he was acting as overseer of the poor, along with George Bell of Beeches, while being a prominent member of the Congregational Chapel.

When Samuel Brunwin died, he had been at Stileman's for 47 years. He was a staunch supporter of the Congregational Chapel and is buried with Susan in the cemetery on Runwell Road.

Until 1850, Wickford Hall and farm was owned by Colonel John Fane, although he himself did not live in Wickford. In 1840 it was under the management of David Archer, who lived in Great Aimes farmhouse with seven servants and allowed Wickford Hall to be occupied by agricultural labourers. Archer continued to farm these two estates, later taking on Barn Hall Farm (then part of Downham

73   John Brewitt of Bridge House Farm died in 1860 and is buried in his family vault at the south door of Downham church.

parish) in addition, and made Wickford Hall his home about 1851. Towards the end of the century Archer became the owner of Shotgate Farm.

Abraham Bell was an early tenant of Broomfields Farm, and served as St Catherine's

74　Samuel Brunwin's tomb in the Congregational cemetery, Runwell Road.

churchwarden for many years. His son, Thomas, was the longest-standing owner-occupier in the parish, living at Beeches Farm where he greatly extended the farmhouse. As Beeches was a relatively small estate, Thomas also farmed Beauchamps Farm and The Wick. Thomas himself had become parish overseer at the age of 20 and, by the time he died in 1895, had held every parish office, as well as being instrumental in the enclosure of Rawreth Shot. He was a generous contributor to the rebuilding of St Catherine's church and a subscriber to the school building fund.

In the absence of landed gentry, these farmers, Brewitt, Brunwin, Bell and Archer, along with the rector, formed the highest rung of Wickford society. All of these families employed house servants, most of whom were young, unmarried women.

Edward Rion Berens was presented to the living of St Catherine's in 1833, by Richard Benyonde Beavoir. He received an annual income of some £950, supplemented by renting out the glebe land to Matthias Wendon and his three sons. In addition, the Rev. Berens received income from land he owned as a private individual. Although he retained the living for 34 years, it is doubtful whether the wealthy Rev. Berens resided for any period of time in the village. In 1841, for example, the rectory was in the care of curate, John Barley and his family, and in 1851 occupied by curate Thomas Griffiths, followed in 1861 by a third curate, Richard Fortescue Purvis.

William Hugo Lukin, born in Dorset in 1830, was the fourth curate to the Rev. Berens at Wickford, but took over the living as rector in 1867. He and his wife Alice had travelled across more of England than most Wickford residents could dream of; Alice herself was from Derbyshire, while their eldest two daughters were born in Wiltshire and Lincolnshire. With three younger daughters and one son, the household included a governess, a cook, a nurse and a housemaid. On becoming rector, Lukin immediately set about improving the rectory, taking out a mortgage to add a dining room with bedrooms above it. The Rev. Lukin was also instrumental in the rebuilding of St Catherine's church, taking out a second mortgage on the rector's stipend, to provide £400 towards the building costs. His 'generosity', however, reduced the value of the living for subsequent rectors, it being worth about £325 p.a. before 1867 and £245 after 1877. The Rev. Lukin remained at Wickford until 1881.

By contrast, the ministers of the Congregational Chapel were appointed and paid by their congregations and, therefore, lived by more modest means. Irishman William Dougan, for example, was minister of the Independent chapel in 1851 and lived opposite it in the tiny thatched cottage known as Guinea Pig Hall, which belonged to Samuel Brunwin. He was

75 Building works on the west side of the Broadway, 1904. These premises opposite Wickford Bridge became Gigney's shop.

followed by the Reverends Nugent, McPhail and Garlick.

The village benefited from the services of two resident surgeons during the 1840s: Anthony Wells, who came from Norfolk, and Colchester Thackthwaite, who had lived in Wickford since the age of ten when his father was the village doctor. Colchester lived in a large house set back from the High Street in two acres of land (later occupied by Dr Marshall). However, Colchester died in 1847 aged 44, leaving his wife Sarah and one-year-old daughter Agnes. The Medical Act of 1858 required the registration of practitioners and it became even more likely that doctors and surgeons in a rural village such as Wickford would hail from elsewhere. By 1861, William

Sage was the local surgeon and also worked as one of the four surgeons to the Billericay Union Workhouse.

The Essex Police Force came into being in 1839, the first police station in the county being at Billericay. Wickford was initially part of the Rochford Police Division although it later transferred to Billericay Division, and its first resident police officer was William Edwards from Waltham.

He was succeeded by PC Mark Butcher who was born in Gosfield in 1827 and joined Essex Police on 16 February 1854. At Wickford he lived in the police house, a cottage purchased for the purpose in Jersey Gardens, with his wife, Lucy, and four children. He left the Essex County Constabulary on 31 December 1884

76 Wickford's first police house, Jersey Gardens. Notice the County Police sign above the door. The police later operated from a house in Southend Road until the police station was built in London Road in 1966.

77 Wickford Infants School photograph, *c.*1890. Of the 89 people who died in Wickford in 1885, 63 were under five years old.

and moved to premises in Wickford High Street where his wife ran a sweet shop. His police pension was 2s. 6d. per day. Mark Butcher died on 20 February 1914 and is buried in St Catherine's churchyard. A house in Southend Road became the next police house.

Education was not compulsory during the first half of the 19th century and most children's schooling was sporadic at best, dependent on whether their parents had the inclination or the means to afford the fees at small privately-run schools, if schools existed at all. Wickford's children were fortunate in that most children between the ages of five and 12 seem to have received at least some education.

Widower Edward Crow was a village schoolmaster in 1841. He lived with his sons Joseph, 12, and Walter, 10, a 12-year-old girl as a housemaid and a lodger, 81-year-old Eliza Norfolk. Miriam Crow kept an infant school in a tenement between the bridge and the *Castle Inn*, and Maria Eaton, who lodged at Henry Perry's shoemaker's shop, worked as a teacher of a private school in 1861. Eliza Flack, wife of grocer Daniel Flack, although a married woman, also worked as a schoolmistress, running her school from a room adjoining John Salmon's grocer's shop near Wickford Bridge. When the church school was built in 1861, she was employed as the first mistress there. The Misses Archer remembered Mrs Flack as 'a dear old lady' who, when she considered the use of the cane was necessary, preferred not to deliver the punishment herself but sent for the rector to administer it.

Perhaps the most interesting educational experience was found at a detached house in the High Street where Richard Wallis Champion and his wife, Mary Ann, ran a school. While most of their neighbours remained in the same job their whole lives, the Champions enjoyed a wide variety of employments; Mary Ann, for example, is listed in the census returns as a schoolmistress and also as running a fancy

78 Wickford Junior School photograph, c.1890.

goods shop. Richard appears as a schoolmaster but is also a stationer in various trade directories and, towards the end of his life, was employed as a gardener. Their school, in 1851, included two girls from Ramsden Bellhouse who boarded with the Champion family. Their son James Champion became a farmer's assistant, and daughter Sarah herself became a school teacher.

In 1812, the churchwarden of St Catherine's paid five shillings for a journey to Billericay to 'bind Thomas Reed an apprentice to his uncle Mr Thomas Reed a blacksmith' at his foundry on the corner of the High Street. By the 1840s, Reed also employed two young men who lived with the family and worked in the smithy. The village blacksmith was key to the village economy where so many livelihoods depended on agriculture and agriculture depended on horses. The smith shoed the horses as well as making the implements they hauled.

There were no manufacturers of agricultural machinery in Essex until the end of the century and, before then, landowners or farmers would design their own ploughs, harrows, and so on and ask the local blacksmith to make it for them. Horses were also the primary means of transport, and, in their capacity as farriers, smiths treated animals that fell ill. A good smith could correct faults in a horse's feet. Blacksmiths also worked for fellow villagers making and repairing hoes, scythes, hooks, kettles, pots and pans. Not surprisingly, the smithy often became a general meeting place as men waited for their horses to be attended to.

Thomas Reed would have worked closely with his brother, William, who came to the village to work as a wheelwright. The care of horses and wagons required the joint skills of blacksmiths and wheelwrights and the two craftsmen would often work together, for

79	Broadway shops, c.1900. The shop far right is Gigney's drapers. The weather-boarded cottage on the left was demolished c.1905.

example, the smith making the iron rims for the wright's cart wheels.

The Upson family began as farmers in Wickford, with John Upson tenanting Sappers farm. George Upson jun., however, worked as a saddler and harness maker all his life, beginning in premises opposite the end of Swan Lane and later moving to a workshop in the High Street. His family lived in a house near the railway bridge.

Saddlers produced collars and harnesses for horses as well as headstalls, halters, and hemp plough reins or cords. Obviously, their main material was leather, but George Upson would also have used metal for buckles, hooks, chains and bits, wood for the frame of cart saddles, straw for stuffing, flock for padding and woollen cloth for lining collars. For most of the 19th

century, the horse was the most important item a farmer owned and, therefore, saddlers were vital, as harnesses needed almost constant repair. When self-binder harvesting machines came into use, some saddlers repaired the canvas conveyor-belts which delivered the sheaf of corn after it had been tied.

David Upson, also a harness maker, served as both parish clerk and sexton during his lifetime, retiring to a cottage on the London Road.

James Gigney, originally from Burnham, set up a saddlery business in 1837, living near the Wickford Bridge with his wife Mary and Susannah (possibly his sister-in-law). He expanded his business to become a saddler and ironmonger, employing four men, plus his own younger brother, Michael, in premises on the west side of the Broadway. James' wife Mary

Cement Fire Clay Goods, Galvanized Iron, Etc.

THE HARDWARE STORES,

ESTABLISHED 1837.

WICKFORD, ESSEX.

JAMES GIGNEY,

Saddler and Harness Maker,

IRONMONGER AND UPHOLSTERER,

Dealer in CHINA, GLASS and EARTHENWARE.

STACK AND WAGON COVERS, Sacks, all sorts. **OILS & COLORS,** NOSE BAGS, COCOA MATTING and Brushes.

NAILS, TRACE, PITCH, TAR & GREASE, Bean Ties & Spun Yarn, **WAGON ROPES,** AND Plough Lines.

Ready-made Clothes, Boots and Shoes, Garden and other Seeds.

AGENT FOR GUARDIAN FIRE AND LIFE OFFICE, THE RAILWAY PASSENGERS' ACCIDENT COMPANY, SINGERS' SEWING MACHINES, AND BRADFORD'S MANGLES.

All kinds of Timber, Scantlings, Match and Feather E lge Boards. Lime, Cement, Sand and Builders' Materials of all descriptions.

J.G. is prepared to undertake the **REMOVAL OF FURNITURE,** &c., on SPRING VANS.

ESTIMATES GIVEN FOR GENERAL CARTAGE, EITHER BY DAY OR JOB.

SACKS LENT ON HIRE.   SALES ATTENDED AND GOODS BOUGHT ON COMMISSION.

80 Advertisement for James Gigney's many services.

died in 1847, aged 31, very soon after the birth of their son John. Baby John himself died one year later. James then married Susannah and was blessed with a son James and twin daughters, Ada and Ida.

James Gigney jun. was born above the family shop on 15 October 1853 and went on to take over the family business, expanding into ironmongery and grocery, also building and renting out some cottages. Sporting a large moustache and sideburns, he became an important and philanthropic member of the community, being one of the first parish councillors, active in improving water and lighting supplies to the village, and a churchwarden of the Congregational Chapel.

Shoemaker Joseph Crow served as a deacon of the Congregational Chapel for 40 years. In fact, it was probably Joseph who donated the small plot of land on which the first chapel was built as it adjoined his own property. He died in 1837, leaving a widow, Ann, who took over the shoemaking business while their daughter,

Naomi, worked as a governess and later ran a school for girls from her cottage opposite Stileman's. Ann was able to supplement her income by renting out three fields she owned, and died in 1860.

Surprisingly, a shoemaker's work in rural areas was often seasonal, with orders for boots and shoes coinciding with the receipt of harvest wages. During the rest of the year there was little left over from a labourer's wages after the weekly food had been purchased for luxuries such as shoes for children. The leather of new boots was very stiff and uncomfortable until softened by liberal applications of oil. Other shoemakers in the 19th-century village were John Riley, Henry Perry, William Moyse, who lived next to the village pump, and William Emery.

Innkeeper Robert White died in 1835 and was buried in St Catherine's churchyard where his gravestone confirms that he performed his duties 'upwards of 20 years with credit to himself and satisfaction to all his neighbours'.

81 Cigar Box and the *Castle Hotel*. The Cigar Box was pulled down to make way for the pedestrian underpass.

In fact, records show that White had been landlord of the *Castle* since at least 1800. He was thought of as a kind and indulgent father. Samuel Bridge from Maldon became the village's next innkeeper, later retiring to a cottage almost opposite the *Castle*, next to the village pump. Subsequently, the *Castle Inn* became the home of Reuben Dines, his wife Lucy, seven children, two servants and four lodgers.

Opposite the *Castle* was a row of cottages owned by Thomas Bell, which included the baker's shop where George Salmon (b.1818) lived and worked, supporting not only his wife Sarah and four children, but also two young house servants. Although many people made at least some of their own bread, scarcity of fuel and lack of suitable ovens in many cottages ensured a brisk trade for the village baker.

Next door, old William Rushbrook died in his cottage in 1841; he had worked as the

village vet for 40 years, and beyond him lived 65-year-old William Woollard the wheelwright with his wife Ann, son William and ten-year-old wheelwright's apprentice John Clark. William Woollard jun. took over his father's business and became successful enough to employ two men and an apprentice, as well as supporting his widowed mother. However, William died in February 1861 aged 50, leaving his wife Elizabeth to take over his business to support their children Myra, 16, and eight-year-old George. The misfortune became a tragedy a year later when young Myra died in June 1862, followed four months later by her mother, George Woollard thus becoming an only child and then an orphan at the age of nine.

The name Carter appears in Wickford records from the early 19th century, and the 1861 census records no fewer than nine households with the surname Carter. In 1841, builder John Carter and his wife Martha lived next door to the Woollards, in a modest brick-built dwelling, later rebuilt as the *Swan Inn*. Martha was one of the few married women in the village with occupations of their own and worked as a straw bonnet maker. This was a popular cottage industry in Essex during the 19th century when all 'respectable' people wore some kind of head covering, and in rural areas straw hats were the choice of both men and women. Bonnet making was mainly carried on by women working from home with plaits of straw woven together and shaped over a block of plaster or wood. Bonnet makers would also clean or re-block old hats. The heyday of the industry was 1850-80, after which it declined rapidly because of cheap foreign imports.

Another John Carter was building up his carpenter's business in Wickford in 1841. He lived with his wife Elizabeth and their sons,

Thomas, George, John, Samuel, Joseph and David. By 1861, John Carter had diversified into building work, but two of his sons still worked as carpenters, as did John's two lodgers.

Jacob Carter also worked as a carpenter in the village. Carpenters had much domestic work to do, repairing and constructing window frames, doors and cupboards, and making and mending furniture. However, like the saddlers and wheelwrights, they were likely to gain the greater part of their livelihoods from the farms, where there were gates to make, outbuildings to repair, cow-cribs, pig troughs and ladders to construct.

George Carter, aged 27, was working as a bricklayer in 1861. George was married to Hannah and was a father to Frederick and Hannah Jane. In 1863 this family celebrated the birth of a second daughter, Louisa, but the

82 Broadway, looking north from the railway bridge on a Monday morning. These gentlemen are in town to visit the market.

83 View from the railway bridge, *c.*1905.

minister noted in the parish register against the record of baptism for Louisa: 'Father deceased one month after birth of child'. Widow Hannah became a mangle woman to support the family and took in two lodgers.

Samuel White, born in Downham in 1804, had joining the military and met his Irish wife, Ann, in Dublin. Soon after the birth of his two sons, Samuel became a Chelsea Pensioner and brought his family to Wickford for his retirement. The younger children, two girls, were still at school when Ann was widowed. She lived just east of Wickford Bridge and worked in a shop and, after it was built in 1861, also acted as a caretaker for the schoolroom at £2 per annum. Her eldest child, James, an agricultural labourer, was caretaker of the Congregational Chapel for many years, while son Samuel jun. followed his father's career and became a private in the Essex Militia. When James married, his mother moved in with him and his young family while taking

in work as a dressmaker. She would only have made clothes for women and girls, while their male relatives would use a tailor. Interestingly, Wickford did not have its own tailor and would have relied on journeymen visiting the village. Tailors made anything from the breeches, jackets and overcoats worn by farmers to the heavy cord trousers and waistcoats favoured by their labourers.

Large families were common and John North worked hard as a painter to support his wife, Mary, and their seven daughters. He often undertook work on behalf of the churchwarden, with duties including: painting the church gates, nine shillings, painting and whitewashing the church, £5 10s. During the 1850s, John North expanded his painting business into plumbing, while his wife Mary worked as a milliner and dressmaker and two of his daughters made straw bonnets. However, by 1861, Mary was a widow living alone but still running the painting business with two men working for her.

Charles Pepper began his working life as a farmboy on Great Aimes farm but, by 1861, was an agricultural labourer supporting a wife and six children while his father-in-law, Jeremiah Aves, still contributed to the family income as an agricultural labourer at the age of 75. Son James, 16, was earning his own living working as a groom for David Archer at Wickford Hall Farm. James Pepper, however, was not the youngest employee in the village in 1861. His younger sister, Martha, was working as a domestic servant for the Congregational minister by the age of 14. George Elsdon, a drover, was only 13 years old, and house servant George Chandler was only 12 years old.

Other humble members of the community included Maria Cockley, widowed in 1840, who lived with ten-year-old Emma Chambers. Her sons were agricultural labourers: Thomas, who lived and worked on Broomfields Farm,

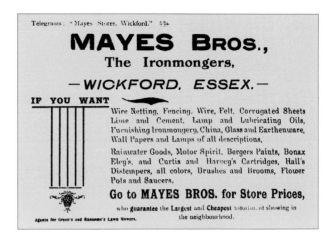

84 Mayes Brothers advertisement, 1915.

and John who shared a cottage with his wife Margaret. By 1861, John Cockley had become disabled and would have been dependent on the generosity of his neighbours for parish relief of two or three shillings a week. However, by

85 George English's post office. By 1900 the postmaster was dealing with three collections and deliveries each weekday. From 1890-1924 the local postman was William Bearman.

87 The Bartlett family outside Orchard Cottage, Runwell Road, *c.*1880.

86 Franklin's butchers in the Broadway had its own slaughterhouse behind the shop.

1871, John is again recorded as an agricultural labourer, suggesting that his disability had been only temporary.

James Punt (b.1767) appears on the lists of ratepayers in the late 18th century as the tenant farmer of Stileman's and even, in 1785, served as parish overseer. However, his fortunes changed after the death of his wife and, in 1821, he was sentenced to one month's hard labour and whipping for 'intention to steal'.

By 1841 he was living near Nevendon Bridge with his son, James jun., daughter-in-law and seven grandchildren and, aged 74, was working as an agricultural labourer. Cottages in this area were among the poorest in the village, being subject to regular flooding. The family had lost at least one baby, David, who died in 1830, but the high infant mortality rate at the time made it more unusual that James Punt senior was a grand old age of 77 when he passed away in 1844.

About 1850, Richard Digby and his wife lived in the same area, just over the Nevendon Bridge, in a small dwelling that was formerly a caravan at a rent of one shilling a week. The property was purchased by the Rev. Davies when he made the entrance to Wick Drive.

Moses Miller married Love Archer of Rayleigh in 1814 at the age of 28 and opened a grocery shop in Wickford Broadway, just north of the bridge. Shops were a valuable resource when a journey to town was a rare event for a poor villager, although it was common for the grocer to be offered produce rather than money for his goods. Shelves would be stocked with cheese, bacon, tea, butter, sugar and treacle, as well as drapery, matting, ironmongery and candles.

In 1832, Miller became the first village postmaster. His responsibilities included sorting the Wickford mail for local distribution by the postman whose daily journey stretched from Battlesbridge to North Benfleet via Runwell and Wickford. People could leave outgoing mail at the post office and Miller would ensure its despatch to Billericay at 6.45 each evening. Miller outlived his second wife, Frances, and became one of the very few Wickford residents who lived all alone.

Benjamin Franklin, a butcher, was also widowed at an early age but went on to marry Elizabeth Bridge in 1831, with whom he had at least eight children. The village butcher would slaughter his own meat, often in an outhouse behind the shop, and most of his trade was local. In addition to meat, Franklin no doubt sold a large quantity of lard and dripping to his poorer customers.

Richard Bartlett worked as a cattle dealer from his house on the Runwell Road to support his household, which consisted of his wife Mary, children James and Sarah and granddaughter Sarah Mansfield. Richard Bartlett was widowed in 1860, but his granddaughter Sarah continued to live with him as his housekeeper. A close neighbour was his son, James, who had married his niece, Mary, 45 years his junior.

A generation previously, the Bartlett family had been agricultural labourers. However, those were the days before Wickford had its own market, and the Bartletts' willingness to travel and drove cattle enabled them to build up enough wealth to become landowners. James Bartlett sold a piece of land in the High Street

88 High Street, *c.*1920. The High Street was largely residential until the 1930s. Dr Marshall's house is behind the hedge on the left of this picture.

to the Congregationalists for the building of their new chapel.

Death in early childhood was common, but disease was a real concern for all ages. In 1854 the population of the village dropped significantly during a prolonged outbreak of cholera. Samuel Mason, however, who lived on the corner of Oak Avenue, was gored to death by a bull, leaving a wife and six children.

The people of 19th-century Wickford, therefore, were a diverse community – some 12-year-olds were at school while others were already in full-time employment. Many died in childhood, and few reached their 80s or 90s. Most lived in large family groups, regardless of the size of their homes. A few owned large acreages of land and employed several servants, while most scraped a living on a few shillings a week. However, the rural location of the village and the theme of agriculture bound them together: labourers and craftsmen were dependent on farmers for employment; farmers were dependent on their workers; tradesmen required farmers to do well to bring money into the village. When agriculture thrived, the village thrived.

Seven

Progress

The twenty years either side of 1900 were to prove a turning point for Wickford, as it emerged from being a cohesive, if poor, agricultural community into one with a far greater range of services and facilities but also one with many more conflicts of interest between the residents.

The Railway

During the 1880s Wickford people were paying 23s. a ton for coal plus one shilling a mile for its transportation from a wharf at Battlesbridge. A railway, locals thought, would cut these costs by about a quarter. Furthermore, Rev. Beresford Harris, Rector of Runwell, explained that to get to London by midday he had to be up at 7.30a.m. to catch the 8.20a.m. from Pitsea. The next train did not leave until 11.52a.m., while the last train returning to Southend left London at 7.54 in the evening.

Fortunately for the Rev. Harris, the Great Eastern Railway decided to build a line to Southend sometime between 1875 and 1882. They first proposed to run the track from the existing line at Ingatestone to Stock and thence to Wickford, Rayleigh, Rochford and Prittlewell. However, it was eventually agreed that the line should take in Billericay and include a branch line from Wickford to Southminster and another to Woodham Ferrers and Maldon, with a triangular junction at Wickford. The proposals resulted in an Act of Parliament dated 16 July 1883, defeating competitive schemes put forward by the London, Tilbury

and Southend Railway company to run a line via North Benfleet, and another proposal from the Mid-Essex Railway for a line from Pitsea, via Billericay, to Ingatestone.

Construction entailed building a large embankment and a bridge across Wickford High Street, dividing The Broadway off as a separate road. The line went through the village allotments and several buildings were demolished. In 1882, four acres of Wickford's glebe land was sold to the Great Eastern Railway to allow the building of the Burnham branch line. The church used the money from this sale to build two glebe cottages in Wick Lane.

The first section of the GER line, as far as Shenfield station, opened on 1 January 1887. The foundation stone of Wickford station was laid by the Rev. Beresford Harris, along with Mr W.J. Beard, MP for mid-Essex, and the station opened on 24 June 1887.

It was built with two platforms, two waiting rooms and two signal boxes, one for the main line and one controlling the Southminster branch line. There was a large goods yard and, until the early 1950s, a small locomotive depot. The locomotive yard had a turntable so that steam engines could be turned around for return journeys. At one time, when carriages were lit by gas, there was a gas-making plant at the rear of the 'up' (to London) side platform. The first stationmaster was Thomas Locking.

The section of track from Shenfield to Wickford was opened for goods traffic on

89 Engineers constructing the railway line at Wickford. The *Castle* landlord James Ruffhead would obtain a late licence to provide supper for the workers.

19 November 1888. However, major excitement was reserved for 7.30a.m. on 1 January 1889, when two ladies and a policeman left Wickford for Shenfield on the first passenger train. Later that day, a special train from Liverpool Street carried directors and officials of the Great Eastern Railway to Wickford and thence back to Billericay for a public luncheon. People lined bridges, platforms and station approaches to cheer the train on its way and a celebration was held at the *Castle Inn*.

Initially, there were five trains a day, on Mondays, Tuesdays and Thursdays in each direction between Shenfield and Wickford, and six trains every day on Wednesdays, Fridays and Saturdays. By 1911 there were six non-stop

90 Station foundation stone laid on 24 June 1887 by the Rev. Beresford Harris, rector of Runwell, who had campaigned for the railway.

91   Wickford railway station, with a train approaching from London. Note the milk churns waiting for collection on the 'up' platform.

92   Railway engineers and station staff, *c.*1900.

93 Looking south through the railway bridge, *c.*1900. The man holding the horse is Mr Harvey the coal merchant. The bridge split the High Street, creating the Broadway, and was replaced with a new bridge in February 1988.

trains a day to London, with some fast trains managing the journey in less than an hour, although most took slightly longer.

Wickford station became known as Wickford Junction when the single track branch from Wickford to Southminster opened in June 1889, and a cottage was built in Wick Lane for the crossing keeper.

The section from Wickford to Southend opened that same year, together with a curve from Fanton signal box (between Wickford and Rayleigh) to the Southminster branch. When the first train on the new line section left Southend, it was cheered along its journey. It heralded the end of the last stagecoach. In the early days, there was only one train a day from Southend to Liverpool Street and the line's main traffic was agricultural produce, bricks and

coal. However, by 1910 up to 31,000 people travelled from London to Southend via the GER on a Bank Holiday weekend.

In 1896 the railway line between Prittlewell and Rochford was doubled and, in 1901, the section from Rochford to Wickford was similarly doubled.

Train fares quickly became a contentious issue and in 1903 the Rev. Dormer Pierce in his capacity as Chairman of the Parish Council proposed that the railway company be asked to make the return fare from Wickford to Southend the same as from Southend to Wickford, i.e. 1s. 1d.

In 1907, a two-acre plot of land behind the High Street, often used for village cricket matches, was purchased from Wells & Perry Brewery, owners of the *Castle Inn*, and 12,800

94   Shotgate railway bridge. The road beneath the bridge had to be lowered to accommodate high vehicles.

cubic yards of earth was dug out to make a reservoir of two million gallons of water for use by the steam trains.

Parish Council

1894 saw the establishment of Urban and Rural District Councils, which took over the administration of local affairs from the vestry meetings. Billericay became a Rural District Council, with 25 parish councils, including Wickford, within its jurisdiction.

A meeting held at the *Castle Inn* on 4 December 1894 agreed that a poll to elect parish councillors should be held on

95   Wick Lane railway crossing. If you wanted to cross the line with a horse and cart, you had to ask at the cottage for the gate to be unlocked.

96 Wickford station became known as Wickford Junction when the branch line to Southminster opened in 1889.

17 December. However, when that date arrived, only seven candidates offered themselves for office, and they were elected uncontested. Wickford's first Parish Council, therefore, comprised farmer William Archer, grocer and draper George English, butcher Henry Franklin, saddler and ironmonger James Gigney, grocer and baker George Hellen Patmore, publican James Ruffhead and market gardener Albon Skeels. Thus, the responsibility for the day-to-day administration of the parish passed out of the hands of the local farmers and into those of the village tradesmen.

The first official meeting of the new Parish Council took place on 18 December at the school when the Rev. Porter accepted the position of Chairman of the Council, with George Patmore as vice-chairman, and James Gigney as treasurer. David Upson, already fulfilling the post of parish assistant overseer, was to act as Clerk to the Council.

The first action the new Council took was at their second meeting, 9 January 1895, when they proposed a letter to the highways surveyor at Essex County Council asking him to lop the trees overhanging the Southend Road. They also initiated enquiries into the ownership of land known as Wickford Green opposite the *Swan Inn*, subsequently found to belong to Thomas Bell, and into the feasibility of providing lighting for the village.

Although 11 sites were quickly identified as being in need of lamps, and a sub-committee was set up to take responsibility for lighting, the question of lamp suppliers, purchase of benzene and maintenance of the lamps preoccupied the Parish Council for several years. James Gigney undertook to provide and maintain a lamp outside his own premises in the Broadway. The Great Eastern Railway Company, however, refused to provide an additional lamp at the entrance to the station despite the opinion of the Council that 'it is on a dark night a very dangerous place'.

The third meeting of the Parish Council decided, unfortunately for local historians, that it was unnecessary to keep the old rate books and that they should be burnt. Other documents, however, were to be 'deposited in a box and kept in a convenient place'. Meetings continued to take place at the village school, although after 1898 they

97   Robert True's drapers, High Street. Robert True served as a deacon of the Congregational Chapel for over 40 years. In 1934 he stood the cost of redecorating the chapel inside and out.

occasionally met at the Congregational Chapel reading rooms.

The 1888 Local Government Bill saw the county reorganised into 63 divisions. At this time, those fields lying in the angle between the London Road and High Street belonging to South Hanningfield parish were officially annexed to Wickford. Other fields, belonging to Downham and Runwell, did not become part of Wickford until 1960.

A Village Green

Thomas Bell of Beeches died on 14 April 1895 at the age of 85. He had served as parish overseer at the age of 20 and had held almost every parish office in turn since then. The Parish Council agreed that he had 'served the parish faithfully

and well' and sent a letter of condolence to his family.

Soon after his father's death, Thomas Bell jun. wrote to the Parish Council that the executors of the will were willing to make over to the Parish Council all rights to the strip of land in front of the *Swan Inn* and adjoining premises if the Council would undertake that it should 'not at any time hereafter be built upon, and should always be retained either as an open or ornamental space for the benefit of the inhabitants of Wickford'. The Council proposed to accept the land on the condition named, provided that a portion of the land might be taken into the road for the purpose of improving the highway. Consequently, the conveyance of Mr Bell's plot of land was signed

2 March 1896, and in October that year a strip of this land was handed over to Essex County Council for the purpose of widening the road.

The land was to be used as a parish green and the police constable was instructed to remove any horse or vehicle stationed upon it without the written consent of the Council. By February 1897, the Council had decided that the green be planted with shrubs and protected with a post and chain fence to provide an ornamental public space. This was not universally approved, however. Luker and Co., owners of the *Swan*, which had opened in 1880, wrote disputing the Council's right to enclose the land and James Gigney, whose grocer's shop fronted the green, asserted his right of usage.

Luker's Brewery suggested that the green be granted to them in exchange for a strip of

98 East side of High Street, *c.*1920. The Congregational Chapel is just out of shot on the left; its railings can be seen.

land beside the *Swan Inn* to enable them to extend their building at the front. While some members of the Parish Council felt this was the ideal opportunity to widen Swan Lane at what was agreed to be a dangerous corner,

99 Broadway, with the *Swan* and Harvey's. Harvey's coal merchants and haulage premises were built on the site of three old cottages where the Cockleys, Peppers and Ensons lived and were destroyed by fire in April 1939.

others felt they were breaking their agreement with Thomas Bell.

A manifesto was circulated in the town, with the headline 'God Save the Queen and Wickford', urging parishioners to speak out against giving up one inch of public footway, and local newspapers reported, 'Great has been the internal strife raging at the usually quiet village of Wickford over a small strip of ground situated in front of the *Swan Inn*, Wickford Street'. As Wickford residents know, Thomas Bell's generous bequest to the town of 'an open and ornamental space' in perpetuity has long since been all but forgotten.

Water Supply

In 1883, an official report from Dr Carter, an inspector from Essex County Council, recorded that the water from Wickford's public pump had been analysed and that it had been found 'fairly good … but insufficient'. At the first AGM of Wickford Parish Council on 17 April 1895, James Gigney raised the issue that, together with lighting, was to become the primary concern of the Council for the next few years. He proposed that Billericay Rural District Council be requested to consider making available a further supply of water for the village, pointing out that 'the present supply of water at Wickford is already failing and that it is necessary that immediate steps should be taken for affording the village a further supply.

Billericay RDC replied that if Wickford provided further details, they would consider providing a water supply from Danbury in Chelmsford District. Wickford would have to pay one shilling per thousand gallons for all water supplied at the boundary of the parish, including at least 40,000 gallons per week for the railway company.

100   Rowing boats on the Crouch, *c.*1935. One hundred years ago, kingfishers were common on this stretch of the River Crouch.

When first sunk, the spring that was the source of the water in Wickford's village well had risen to surface level, but in 1900 it only rose to a point some 29 feet below surface level, and the Wickford Parish Sanitary Committee decided to regulate the opening times of the well to three hours in the morning and three in the evening to prevent the supply drying up completely, probably by erecting a fence with lockable gates. They also threatened action against those using obscene language near the well.

However, the Parish Council had heard with 'grave apprehension' a proposal from Billericay RDC to interfere with the parish pump and well, and felt that this would be wasted expenditure. In addition, Dr John Thresh, the County Sanitary Inspector, felt that deepening the well might pollute the existing water supply and wrote in protest against the idea: 'this Council protests as strongly as ever against the deepening of the well', while reiterating support for the alternative supply from Danbury. Billericay RDC replied that, despite any objections, the well was to be deepened at a cost of £46 10s.

Therefore, under the direction of Billericay Council, 1900 saw a new reservoir sunk 18 feet below the working level of the spring head, making the well some 47 feet deep. This produced a supply of some 4,000 gallons in 24 hours.

Work at the well had caused damage to the footpath between the pump and the railway bridge, but when repairs were requested from the County Surveyor, the Parish Council was told 'there is so much muck and dirt about, special work must stand over until we get some dry weather'.

Linked to the diminishing water supply was the problem of the stench from the River Crouch as it passed through the village. In 1899, Robert Thomlinson refused to allow his child to cross the bridge to go to school as he

101 Train fares, 1928.

thought the smell was unhealthy. He was fined five shillings for keeping the child off school, but Dr Thresh agreed that the Crouch was 'foul in the extreme', with the stench particularly bad on hot days. The filters were not cleaned; storm drains were put under pressure and sewage forced its way out of the storm chamber and 'caused a nuisance'. The tank should have been cleaned out two or three times a year but this was hardly ever carried out.

James Gigney independently sought permission from Chelmsford Rural Council to tap the main water pipe from Danbury to the Great Eastern Railway at a rate of three shillings per 1,000 gallons. By 1901 this was supplying the railway and a few neighbouring houses. Gigney charged one penny per four gallons to his customers, with a reduction for large quantities. When 16 householders became infected with disease, Gigney's standpipe was suspected of being polluted but the source of the infection was never established.

102 Train at the station, 1955. The opening of the railway marked an increase in residential population, local businesses and tourism.

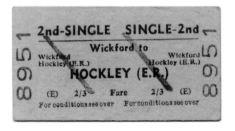

103 Railway tickets, 1967.

In 1904, nine years after it had first been proposed, arrangements were made for a general supply of water to Wickford from Danbury. It was agreed that the pipe from the railway bridge would be extended to the village pump and that a standpipe with two taps be placed by the side of the pump and that water should be available there from 7a.m. to 10a.m. and from 5p.m. to 8p.m. The pump was to be opened on Mondays, Wednesdays and Saturdays only. However, the next meeting of the Parish Council decided that the pump should be closed altogether, and that the villagers would rely on the standpipe.

A year later, the Parish Council informed Billericay RDC that Wickford wished to be connected to Southend Water Company system, which was being laid along the Southend Road. Arthur Darby was contracted to carry out the work using local labour, and the homes fronting Southend Road were connected by the end of 1905.

Water rates were introduced at a rate of 2s. 6d. on a house with a rateable value of £5. More expensive properties paid five pence in the pound. Anyone caught stealing or wasting water, still a valuable commodity, was liable to prosecution and a five-shilling reward was promised to informers. Mr Tilbrook, who lived in Runwell, drove around with a red, white and blue waterbutt nicknamed 'Aquarius', selling water at a halfpenny a bucketful.

In 1907, the Southend Waterworks Company took over all of Wickford's water supplies and it was estimated that five gallons of water per day was being used by each person in the town. Gas mains were laid in the town in 1909.

Many Wickford properties were not connected to the main sewer until the 1930s.

Wickford Bridge

In 1899, the main London to Southend road became the responsibility of Essex County Council, while the local roads remained the responsibility of Billericay Rural District Council. In that year the Parish Council wrote to the Chief Surveyor of Essex County Council regarding the importance of the structural alteration to the bridge leading from the High Street to the Southend Road. The bridge was so old and narrow, they explained, that vehicles could not pass each other and, as traffic along this road had very greatly increased in recent years, 'an alteration of the construction of the bridge is urgently needed ... accidents are extremely likely to occur in the present condition of the bridge especially to children going to and coming from school and to foot passengers generally'. One proposal to accommodate change was the straightening of the river at the bridge.

Beyond the bridge the footpath was so rough in summer and muddy in winter that people preferred to walk in the road, endangering themselves and inconveniencing traffic. In 1901 the High Street was kerbed and a 20mph speed limit set on vehicles. However, in 1905, villagers were still reporting that the footpaths remained 'very unpleasant to walk upon'.

104 Plaque from Wickford Bridge. Following years of complaints from residents, Wickford Bridge was completely rebuilt in 1915. Children were given a half-day off school to watch the opening ceremony.

Discussions with Essex County Council continued from 1901 to 1908, when it was finally decided that widening Wickford Bridge was not essential enough to warrant the expense. In 1911, James Gigney offered to donate the land to enable the work to be done but there was still no public money for it. Mr Halstead made a similar offer in respect of Nevendon Bridge, and met with the same response.

After continued entreaties from the Parish Council and villagers, a new bridge was eventually built in 1915 and on 29 October that year the village children were given time off school to watch the opening ceremony.

Community Spirit

Wickford Cricket Club was formed in 1887 by Richard Patmore, the landlord of the *Swan* (and son of local councillor George Patmore), Seth Franklin and Robert True. A football club followed in 1899, both clubs meeting in an upper room of the *Swan*.

The cricket team first played on Franklin's Field north of the Southend Road and then on a field that was part of Bridge House Farm (then owned by Mr O. Halstead). A few years

105 The *Swan Inn* after it was rebuilt, *c.*1925. Richard Patmore's three sons all died young, and the pub was left to his surviving child, daughter Medeline.

THE "SWAN" INN,
WICKFORD.
(Now fully Licensed).

CHOICEST WINES & SPIRITS,
DINNERS & TEAS provided on the shortest notice.

FIRST-CLASS STABLING AND LOOSE BOXES.
Horses, Traps, Broughams, and Wagonettes,
On hire at moderate charges.

TRAINS MET at the STATION
Proprietor   -   -   -   R. W. PATMORE

106 The *Swan Inn* advertisement.

later they transferred to a field behind the Congregational Chapel until it was purchased by GER to build a reservoir. Finally, about 1905, Richard Patmore purchased a field near Stileman's for £1,600 for the purpose. His daughter, Medeline, inherited the field and donated it to the cricket club.

The Salvation Army was active in the town from the 1890s, with a hall on the Runwell Road, at the furthest extremity of Wickford. They would march into town and play hymns on the green outside the *Swan Inn* at 7p.m., conducted by builder Frank Carter who lived next to their chapel, but it is said that locals were so annoyed by the band that they would beat saucepans and bins to drown out the music, and even throw missiles. Often the Army were chased back to their hall and, once, Seth Franklin put his foot through their big drum.

To celebrate Queen Victoria's Diamond Jubilee in 1897, and the 60th anniversary of his business, James Gigney gave all Wickford's pensioners one pound of free tea. Stilemans' barns were cleared and decorated, and long tables were laid down the middle for a sit-down meal, followed by races and games, including climbing the greasy pole and singing minstrels. Dr and Mrs Marshall also provided a tea for the town's old folks and children.

Eight

Land Sales

Towards the end of the 19th century, farmers were struggling against competition from cheap imports of wheat from Canada and America and a worldwide fall in prices. In the 20 years from 1875, the price of British wheat halved from 50 shillings a quarter to 24 shillings; similarly, land values halved. These falling prices, coupled with several years of poor harvests and higher taxes, threw Essex farmers, many of whom depended on wheat, into severe financial difficulties. In 1897, the Royal Commission of Agriculture reported that 'farmers had for the past 20 years received on average only 60 per cent of the sums which were in past days considered as ordinary and average profit'. There

was a movement of Scottish farmers to Essex, attracted by the falling price of land, and Mr Macleod brought dairy farming to Wickford Hall Farm. Dairy farming took over from arable to a large extent, with fields laid to grass and workers laid off.

Some small farmers turned to market gardening, supplying tomatoes and flowers for the London market. By 1910, five nurseries existed in Wickford, for example, H. Spencer, which supplied the Stratford market, and Mr Cork on Irvon Hill.

In 1900 a meat and livestock market was established in the Broadway just north of the railway bridge opposite the *Castle Hotel*, open

107 Market day, *c.*1910. The market began on this site beside the railway in 1900. It soon expanded into an additional site on the south side of the railway.

108 Market day, *c.*1922. Wickford became known for the sale of small livestock, particularly poultry.

morning and up to Franklin's slaughterhouse, behind his shop in the Broadway, later in the day. The market came to be known for auction sales of cattle and poultry.

New industry came about with the Wickford Brickworks being established on 16 acres on the Nevendon Road. The site was owned by Henry Wood (1899-1906), Daniel Cornish (1906-22) followed by John Cornish, and later by W.T. Lamb and Sons (1929-37). A terrace of cottages for the workers was erected near the present entrance to Wick Drive. Workers dug the clay in winter months and made bricks in the summer, turning out some 1,000 bricks an hour. Bricks from the Nevendon Road works were typically yellow and not as hard-wearing as red bricks and they were often used decoratively with other types of brick. Several houses around

on Mondays. The market soon expanded onto an additional site immediately south of the railway. Conversely, Billericay market closed down completely in 1912. Market days saw cattle being driven down the High Street in the

109 Market day, *c.*1922. The *Castle* benefited from increased trade on Mondays when farmers flocked to town to buy and sell at the market.

110 The market, 1923. From the 1950s, pens were gradually replaced by stalls; the market moved to its present site in 1972.

the northern end of Nevendon Road were built with local bricks. Other Wickford bricks were driven down to Kent where Winston Churchill wanted a particular type of brick to match those in the walls he was repairing at Chartwell. This brickworks continued its production up to the Second World War and did not close completely until the 1960s.

The station sawmill was set up behind the *Swan*, and beyond it another small brickworks. This works had its own tramway to transport bricks directly to the station. There was another brickworks east of Castledon Road.

Housing – Demand and Supply

In April 1896, at the AGM of the Wickford Parish Council, the Rev. Jesse Hawes, Minister of the Congregational Chapel, spoke of the great need for houses in Wickford and moved that the Parish Council lay before the Billericay Rural District Council the urgent need for homes in Wickford to accommodate the working classes. 'In well-known cases,' he said,

'labourers and others of the same social type have to travel long distances from the parish to find accommodation and many families are now waiting for homes in Wickford.' He thought it was nothing short of cruelty that men, having worked hard all day, should have to walk six miles home.

In fact, it was not only those already employed in the town who were looking to

111 Brickfield Cottages, Nevendon Road. These cottages were built with local bricks.

112   Lawn Estate, c.1930. Most of these houses were built by the owners. Note the posts on the right, marking out individual plots still for sale.

make their homes in Wickford. By the end of the 19th century, the extension of the railway network had given many people from the East End of London a glimpse of another life and the hope of a new start in the countryside of Essex. Their dreams were encouraged by the fall in land prices and by property speculators.

Wickford, along with Laindon, Basildon, Pitsea and Benfleet, was particularly attractive to developers. Tracts of land, sometimes whole farming estates, were purchased and divided into individual building plots that were then re-advertised for sale to the public. These so-called 'plotlands' were offered without the benefit of metalled roads, water supply or services of any description – but it was their low price and their availability to those for whom freehold ownership had previously been an unobtainable dream that was their great attraction.

The population of Wickford in 1900 was just over 630 and John Thresh, Essex County Council's Sanitary Inspector, noted that '43 houses have been built and 400 building plots have been sold'. However, Wickford enjoyed a few more years of rural idyll, with H.W. Tompkins recording in 1903 that accents were still so broad that none but a local could understand what Wickford villagers said. Two

113   Elder Avenue, part of the Wickford Avenue Estate.

114 Plotland homes on Elder Avenue, formerly part of Bridge House Farm.

years later, the Rev. Dormer Pierce said of Wickford: 'the land around is undulating, well-wooded and exceedingly pretty'. It was this 'prettiness', coupled with easy access to London provided by the railways and availability of cheap land, that brought about a rapid change to the face of Wickford in the first decade of the new century.

The railway companies actively encouraged the sales of land for, although the impetus for the railway had been the demand from working-class Londoners for day trips to the coast, the railway companies needed a permanent local population if their businesses were to flourish. Therefore, the railway companies co-operated with land agents to run special trains from London to speculative land sales sites. Free lunches, drinks and transport from the railway station became a regular feature of the sales events. George Ramuz, son of Frederic, declared that 'the enterprising and progressive policy of the Great Eastern Company is well known and the company may confidently be expected

to keep well abreast of the growing needs of the district'.

Frederic Ramuz was a prominent figure in the sale of land to individuals. Trading as The Land Company, with offices in London and Southend, Ramuz began buying land on the Essex coast as well as at Rayleigh, Pitsea, Basildon, Laindon, Langdon Hills and Wickford. Estates were divided into plots of 20ft by 100ft and were advertised in London's East End, with purchasers lured by cheap rail fares and luncheon laid on at the sale site. The buildings that sprang up on these plots ranged from suburban villas to huts and sheds only used at weekends. Many of the sales were finalised in the *Castle Inn*, which at this time began to style itself as the *Castle Hotel*.

Wickford was presented to prospective purchasers as a 'popular residential centre' with a busy weekly market, ten miles from Southend, with the Essex Union Hounds meeting at Wickford and a golf course at nearby Hockley. The 'delightfully healthy' and

115 Oak Avenue, Shotgate, was developed on Kings Mead, the site of the *Kings Head* inn.

116 Enfield Road. Roads were often not made up nor services laid on for many years after residents moved in to plotland homes.

picturesque woodland countryside would appeal to 'persons wishing to secure economically the advantages of healthy country life'. Furthermore, Wickford was 'a rapidly developing locality' to be preferred to the 'limited environment' of suburbia.

One of the earliest sales of land in Wickford specifically for the purpose of estate development was that of the Cranfield Park Estate in 1895: '29 valuable freehold sites of from 2 to 5 acres each and three lots having an area of 32 acres, 29 acres and 13 acres' were put up for sale. The sale included the farmhouses Broomfield Lodge, Barstable Cottage and Sappers Lodge, and much of the land that had comprised Sharwards (Quakers) and Sappers farms. The lots were variously described as being suitable for pleasure farms, miniature park sites and model dairy farms. In addition, Lower Park Road and Upper Park Road were laid out with 36 plots 40ft wide and offered for sale by Jarvis & Sons, builders of Stock. Great Wasketts Estate, adjacent to Cranfield Park, was put up for sale in 1901, with plots marketed as smallholdings.

According to the sales brochure on the day of the sale, Wednesday 16 October 1895, 'A

special train will leave Liverpool Street for Wickford at 11.50a.m. ... returning at 6.10p.m.'. First-class return tickets including luncheon could be purchased from the auctioneers for 2s. 6d. Agents for the Cranfield Park sale were Harman Brothers of Cheapside, London. They described Wickford as a utopia of good, cheap, accessible land.

Mr Bennett of the Cranfield Park Estate was invited by the Parish Council to report on what success the proprietors had met in their search for water. He replied that none had been found. However, he had found gypsies camping on the developing estate and the parish clerk consequently wrote to the Rural District Council and the Superintendent of Essex Police to ask if it were possible to have them moved on. In fact, the area was a traditional campsite for gypsies who, while there, would visit local houses selling pegs.

Over 200 people came to the sale of the Wickford Avenue Estate west of Nevendon Road in 1897, with a pony and trap laid on to collect buyers from the railway station and lunch served in a large marquee on the estate. Mr Harman, the salesman, stressed the fact that a water main would soon be laid along the main road from the town and that there were many trains between London and Wickford every day. A new brickfield near the estate would make possible speedy building on plots bought and would reduce transportation expenses. Shop frontages, 20ft by 200ft deep, sold at around £17 while many plots in Grange Avenue of 25ft by 190ft sold at less than £10. The 193 plots sold realised a total of £2,000. Most of the buyers were from the Upton Park, East Ham and Forest Gate areas.

Bridge House Farm was also put up for sale at this time, with its orchards, garden and grounds including nine acres of pastureland, three enclosures of arable and pasture amounting to some 31 acres. However, the farm escaped the property developers' clutches on this occasion and was purchased as a working farm by Mr O. Halstead for £2,720.

In 1899, Alfred Sault sold The Wick farmhouse, its yards, buildings and 211 acres for £2,950. Nine acres of 'building land' was sold in two separate lots.

George Brunwin, son of Samuel, died in 1905 and Stileman's Farm was offered for sale by auction in June 1906, ending the family's 70-year association with the estate. The sale comprised 240 acres, including 95 acres of productive arable and pasture land. However, the marketing focused on the land's potential as 'desirable building sites for the erection of villas', and the fact that it offered 'exceptional opportunities to speculators and builders'. The timber-built and tiled farmhouse included two sitting rooms, a kitchen, dairy, five bedrooms, coal and beer cellars and an attic.

Included in the sale was Croft House, a detached house in the High Street with three acres of garden, paddock and meadows, which became the home of Thomas Darby and later Dr Campbell. Stileman's farmhouse, its yards and outbuildings was taken on as a manufacturing site by Thomas Darby. One hundred and sixty acres were purchased by

117 Stileman's Farm sale catalogue.

Frederic Ramuz, while the Rev. D.J. Davis purchased the site of the cattle market opposite the *Castle* and James Gigney purchased many of the plots fronting the High Street, Broadway and Swan Lane.

Gigney followed the trend of dividing land into plots but, owing to the town centre location, built terraced cottages rather than the detached chalets popular out of town. He allowed two-thirds of the purchase money of his plots to remain on mortgage at 4½ per cent on plots sold for £400 and five per cent on those sold for less than £400.

118 New houses under construction in Wick Drive, which crosses the site of the Nevendon Road brickfields.

1906 saw the sale and development of the 24 plots of Wickford Town Estate, on land formerly part of Wick Farm, while a year later buyers were offered six plots on the Mount Road Estate, part of the Wickford Hall Estate near the church and schools, and one of the few estates with mains drainage. These six plots were offered by the Capital & Counties Land Co. Ltd, complete with houses.

To the north of the railway station, the Wickford Garden Village was planned in 1907 and advertised by The Land Company as a 'healthy, bracing, picturesque' area to live. The countryside was 'of a delightfully undulating character' and was well-timbered with fine avenues of elm trees. The estate, it was claimed, would be suitable for those seeking a quiet retirement or for the city gent. It was also marketed as an investment opportunity; profits, buyers were told, would be 'rapid and certain'. Six plots were bought by *Castle Inn* landlord

James Ruffhead for £180, who also purchased part of Barn Hall Farm.

In 1908, a further 108 acres of Wickford Hall was sold for development and in 1910 a portion of the Bridge House Estate was sold off as 359 plots by Fred Taylor & Sons, with deeds that stipulated that 'no spirituous malt or intoxicating liquor' was to be sold from the plots. The remainder of Wickford Hall and Bridge House Farm land became available for development between the wars.

The Wickford Station Estate was about a mile away from the station, between Barn Hall and Chelmsford Road, and was offered for sale in 1910. Mr J. Allen of Ludgate Circus was responsible for the sale of 1,140 numbered and pegged out plots, each with a 20ft road frontage; just a 10 per cent deposit would secure any plot. Deeds stipulated that no caravans, tents or huts were allowed on any plot.

Another estate developed from 1910 was the Ilgars Estate on Runwell Road, named for its proximity to the old Ilgars Farm.

The burgeoning housing development enabled local businessmen to expand and diversify their trades. Henry George Clark advertised as an estate agent, architect and surveyor, while James Gigney offered a furniture removal service as well as extending his main business to ironmongery, china, glass, earthenware, boots, clothing, seeds, timber, lime cement and building materials. The Dean brothers became coach builders, while David Upson, the parish clerk descended from generations of men involved in farming and farm support industries, became a house and insurance agent.

By 1908, Barclays & Co.'s bank was opening from 1.15p.m. to 3.45p.m. on Mondays primarily for the benefit of those doing business

119   Belmont Avenue before the road was made up.

at the newly established market. The original site of the market, opposite the *Castle Inn*, was sold in 1911 as part of the estate of the Rev. D.J. Davies, along with Irvon Hill Farm, which was advertised as 'ripe for development as a building estate'. However, the market

120   Jersey Gardens.

121   Southend Road, 1930s, looking towards the town centre.

continued to thrive and expanded onto a second site, south of the railway line.

By 1910, Wickford had a population of over one thousand. Most of the new settlers grew their own vegetables and many also kept chickens, selling their surplus eggs to supplement their income. Milk was readily available from the remaining farms, although entrepreneurs were quick to seize a market opportunity and soon the new estates benefited from delivery services. Coal could only be delivered to the plotlands in the summer when the ground was hard and, even then, it was left at the end of the unmade roads for residents to collect in buckets and wheelbarrows. Lack of home deliveries was not seen as a major problem, as plotlander Mr J. Peet remembers: 'You could buy everything you could possibly want at Wickford or Laindon and bring it back on the bus.'

A gazetteer of the 1930s reported that the influx of population has been balanced by an increase in amenities and that 'for those content

with placid countryside through which quiet waters flow, the neighbourhood of Wickford offers tranquillity'.

However, the planned residential utopia was not a complete success, or certainly not within the timescale envisaged by the Parish Council and the land developers. One disadvantage was that Wickford was in direct competition with nearby Southend, which began developing several years earlier than Wickford and had the added attraction of strictly controlled development.

The nature of the estates, with rapid building and many temporary occupants, meant that rates often went unpaid by whole areas of plotlanders and, therefore, local authorities had no money with which to provide services. For several years water was a tap at the end of the street and the roads themselves little more than mud tracks. For many growing up on plotland sites, life was carefree and happy. However, others remember feeling stigmatised for living without drainage, gas or electricity

122 The Broadway, 1930s. The large brick building on the right was Wickford's first bank.

supplies and some found it difficult to 'fit in' with the local children.

Several plots in Wickford were not immediately sold because supply outstripped demand and plots further from the village centre proved unpopular. Sales of land on the Cranfield Park Estate, for example, were still going on in 1910, 13 years after it had first been offered. In addition, travellers and squatters who may have been content just to pitch a tent were putting off more respectable settlers. Some buyers found that they could not afford to

123 Schofield & Martin took over James Gigney's premises in the Broadway.

124   London Road, 1930s.

build on their new acquisition, while others used their site as a holiday home, so that many plots were only occupied at the weekends. However, the rateable value of Wickford increased from £3,706 in 1904 to £9,329 in 1914.

When the Council eventually took over plotland sites and laid roads and services, the street layout often bore no relation to that envisaged by the plotland developers.

Darby Digger

In 1900, Thomas Churchman Darby, a tenant farmer from Pleshey, moved to Wickford and formed his own company, Darby Land Digger Syndicate. There he set up his own foundry to manufacture his invention, the Patent Land Digger, which was already acquiring an international reputation. Darby's original premises were in Russell Gardens where in 1902 he built a row of terraced houses for the

125   Bruce Grove, one of the first roads laid out in Shotgate.

workmen he brought with him from Pleshey.
The factory later moved to the Stileman's works
in Runwell Road, where the company began
making and repairing agricultural equipment
as well as making their own patented Darby
Land Digger.

Darby's design was based upon the theory
that digging would result in better aeration of
the soil than ploughing. His steam digger could
dig in one hour as much as 70 men could do
and some workers were concerned about the
perceived threat to their jobs.

When the Parish Council received a letter
of complaint in November 1906 concerning
the appalling condition of Wick Lane, this was
found to be because six or more Darby Diggers
had used the lane, and the company was called
upon to make good the damage.

The Darby Digger dug to a greater depth
than the usual ploughs and Darby successfully
marketed his machines within Essex through his

126 Darby's Pedestrian Broadside Digger, 1879. The
Darby Digger could do the work of 70 men.

offices in Wickford and Billiter Square, London.
Some were sold in South Africa, Canada and
Egypt. The machines manufactured in Wickford
were of a rotary screw design that could be
attached to a traction engine of any make.
They cost about £350 and were exhibited

127 Swan Lane. The sign advertises Sidney C. Darby, Agricultural Engineer, Wickford.

before royalty at York. One of the last Darby Diggers constructed was viewed by George V at the Bristol Royal Show in 1913. However, the machine was very heavy and early models were unreliable and needed a blacksmith to replace broken parts. These factors limited the success of the machine and they failed to sell in large numbers, involving the company in heavy losses. In fact, the Darby's Pedestrian Digger Co. lost in excess of £100,000. Darby's son, Sidney, recalled: 'Round about 1907, it was very hard work trying to sell farm machinery owing to price cutting by dealers and the extended credit required by farmers ...'.

Thomas Darby died in Wickford in 1917 aged 75. His son, Sidney, took over Stileman's works and became a machinery agent and car salesman. By 1930, he had developed a good trade in secondhand farm machinery and became an agent for Fordson and International Junior Tractors, at the same time perfecting the Darby 'all-weather wheels' for tractors and bringing a certain amount of renown to Wickford as a town specialising in the sale of agricultural machinery.

The firm continued to expand and, in 1943, was a stockist of Massey-Harris, David Brown and Fordson tractors. In 1952, still operating from Wickford, Darby added a Leyland diesel generator to his range and, at the 1953 Orsett show, exhibited a British-built crawler tractor, the International D-TD6.

Nine

War and Peace

The early 20th century saw Wickford develop from a tiny agricultural village into a small town, supporting an increasing range of businesses. New residents moving onto the plotland sites created a demand for school places, jobs, shops and public transport. The face of Wickford was changing for ever.

Village Affairs

On 2 October 1901, the Bishop of Barking dedicated a Parish Mission Room on the London Road, for the benefit of those living in the west of the parish. Made of red brick and with a wooden porch, it was 40ft by 18ft and could hold 130 people. It was licensed for divine service, but was subsequently replaced by the building of St Andrew's church, the original mission room becoming the church hall.

Wickford survived a smallpox epidemic in 1902 when extra tents had to be purchased from Billericay, and suffered with serious outbreaks of croup, bronchitis and diphtheria during 1905-6. In 1907 the school logbook recorded that several children had returned to school after six months off with whooping cough.

A Ratepayers Association was formed with 15 members in 1904. On 28 June 1905 parishioners celebrated the 600th anniversary of the

128 The Mission Hall, London Road, built in 1901 and now used as a church hall. It was replaced by St Andrew's church in 1935 (rebuilt 1964), which was dedicated as its own parish in 1980 when the Team Parish of Wickford and Runwell was formed.

129 Public Hall, Jersey Gardens, built by shareholders in 1908 for £500 to accommodate 300 people. It was used as a cinema for a few years and served as a gymnasium and meeting hall. The sign on the opposite street corner advertises land for sale at 32s. 6d. per foot.

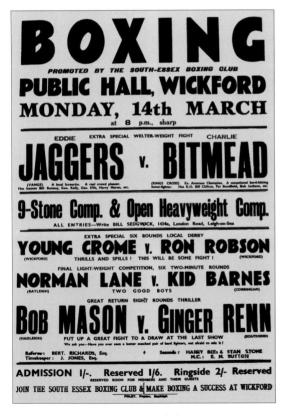

130 Boxing was just one of the many activities taking place in Wickford's Public Hall.

institution of the first rector of St Catherine's with a special service attended by the Bishop of St Albans. At this service a new organ was dedicated.

Season tickets for commuters from Wickford to London in 1910 cost £3 15s. 3d. per quarter or 10d. per day. However, the Parish Council received a letter from Little Burstead Parish Council in April 1926 asking for support in their protest against any increases in the railway fares. The letter stated that the present fares were 'an injustice ... to the railway travelling public of the area' and that, in view of the increasing custom the railway companies were receiving from the expanding commuter population, 'a reduction in fares is more to be expected'. No doubt many current residents of the area continue to support this view. The line was taken over by British Rail in 1948 and electrified from January 1957.

When George V was crowned in 1910, the children of Wickford were each given a medal and a mug to celebrate. Decorated vehicles paraded from Bridge House Farm through

131 Wick Lane junction, clearly signposted 'To Wick Estate only'.

the town, followed by sports, a bonfire and fireworks.

Education

John Henry Gornall was appointed headmaster of Wickford School in 1898 on a salary of £93 a year, with his wife acting as assistant teacher. The 1902 Education Act saw the County Council take responsibility for the administration of the school via an elected committee, or 'board', of local ratepayers. Mr Halstead was appointed manager of the school while the rector, the Rev. Dormer-Pierce, became Chairman of the Managers. The 1905 Essex Local Education Authority inspectors' report declared that the children were 'well-disciplined and taught'. About the same time, Wickford Sanitary Committee recommended that a playground should be provided at the school as the children had to play in the street, but a playground was not available until February 1907.

In 1906, Wickford National School No. 7034 became Wickford Church of England School No. 407. To accommodate increasing pupil numbers, a new classroom was erected in 1907 at a cost of £249, raised by the ratepayers contributing four pence in the pound. There were 156 pupils on the roll in January 1908. The school became used as a meeting place with evening cinematograph entertainments, meetings of the Navy League and the Parish Council.

Soon after the start of the school day on Friday 11 January 1908, Percy Neville, working in his garden near the school, noticed smoke coming from the thatched roof and ran to raise the alarm. The headmaster, John Gornall, marshalled the children out and sent them home. Some builders working nearby came to assist and removed a great portion of the school furniture as well as furniture and personal effects from the headmaster's thatched house adjoining the school. Mrs Gornall had taken

132   Captain F. Plantin with members of Wickford's first fire brigade, formed in 1928.

the day off ill and was in bed at the time; she was carried out to the house of a neighbour (Mr Heslop), while her furniture was stacked in the street.

The fire brigade at Chelmsford was sent for. However, the telegram 'Schools on fire, come at once: Wickford' did not have a signature and the chief officer of the Chelmsford brigade, Cuthbert Brown, unsure as to who would pay the expenses, decided not to turn out.

Instead, the Great Burstead fire brigade led by 2nd Officer Wheeler arrived at 10.45a.m., with their horse-drawn manual fire engine. At Crays Hill, children came out of the school to help push the engine up the hill, but apparently withdrew their support when they learnt that it was attending a school fire. By the time the fire engine arrived and had begun to pump water from a nearby pond, there was nothing left of Wickford School but the brick walls and

some window frames. The destruction included the new classroom, completed just a few weeks earlier. Although the Rev. Dormer Pierce told the press that the event was a 'parochial disaster', his comment in the minutes of the next parish meeting was brief and sanguine: 'The meeting was held at the Mission Room owing to the school having been destroyed by fire.'

It is not clear how the fire had started. Possibly, a spark or a piece of burning paper from the chimney had blown onto the thatch. The school had only just reopened after a measles epidemic, but there were no further lessons for the children until 3 February when James Ruffhead loaned the use of a room on the corner of Jersey Gardens and Station Avenue. Despite £95 being spent on preparing this building for use, a gale in March 'carried a window away'. It proved to be a bad year for Mr and Mrs Gornall and, before they could take up their posts in the new school building, they were asked for their resignations as a result of a disagreement with the school managers over the needlework accounts.

Plans for a new school on the site of the old were drawn up by County Architect Mr Whitmore, and a tender of £754 was accepted from builder Mr T. Raynor of East Hanningfield. The eventual cost, however, came to £900 (£792 of which came from the insurance and £140 was raised by public subscriptions). The new buildings were described in the press as having a 'very bright and cheerful appearance', as well as being 'handsome buildings with all the latest educational improvements'. There was room for 160 children, although there were already 175 children on the roll. Accommodation included a room for the infants of 25ft 6in by 17ft, a room for mixed juniors of 63ft by 16ft, and a six-roomed house for the master. A school motto was adopted: 'Work, civility, obedience, energy mean success'.

The patron of the church, the Rt Hon. Viscount Middleton (St John Broderick),

133 High Street, looking south, c.1930. The gate on the left leads to Dr Robert Frew's house, Ladybrow. Dr Frew served the town for 50 years and is buried in St Catherine's churchyard.

accepted an invitation to open the new school officially on 29 September 1909, when the main schoolroom was decorated with flags and flowers and filled with well-wishers. Viscount Middleton hoped that the magnificent weather with which they had been favoured that day 'might be a forerunner of the relations between those who had to

134 High Street, looking north, c.1930.

work in the school and those who were educated there'.

However, relations were obviously not sunny later that year when the inspectors reported that 'discipline in the infants class is bad'. That same year the school toilets were condemned and the water supply declared inadequate. No wonder that the school logbook reports regular outbreaks of croup, bronchitis, whooping cough, diphtheria, measles, ringworm and chickenpox amongst the pupils. The schools were connected to the main sewer in December 1909. However, in 1920, the caretaker refused to clean the toilets as his 3s. 6d. per month rise had not been paid, and the neighbours began to complain of the smell.

When the school was under the leadership of Mr P.H. Etches in 1910, the inspector's report stated that 'when the master was appointed, the school was in a backwards state – the work is still below average [but] considerable progress has been made'.

In March 1914, despite the town's new drainage system installed in 1905, Mr Harvey's cart was chartered to ferry children to school across floods in the Southend Road. Children from outlying districts were brought in by horse-drawn wagon each day, although children from Nevendon were asked to walk to school 'to save overcrowding on the conveyance'.

It was not long before concern over the rapid population increase led many residents to call for an additional school. Other villagers lodged an appeal against a new school, worried about an increase in the rates. Despite the concerns of this latter group, a new school was opened in Market Road on 14 September 1914 to 'relieve the overcrowding at Wickford Church school, to accommodate children from the parishes of Nevendon and Runwell (where the small schools have now been closed) and to meet the needs of the parishes of Wickford and Downham'.

The new school (now used as the Wickford Infants School) was built for four staff and 130 pupils, with potential to expand to accept a further forty. The formal classrooms were supplemented by additional rooms for cookery and carpentry. On the first day, 105 children were registered, and by 11 November 1914 the school was full with 147 pupils, and three children had to be denied admission. The headmaster was Mr J.C. Davey, assisted by two uncertified teachers and his wife.

In 1919, Archibald Bullock became the new headmaster of the church school in Southend Road. He reported that the place was untidy, with cobwebs around the rooms and old kettles and pans lying about the premises. The work standards were 'shocking, disgraceful and very bad'. The children were said to be unruly and disobedient and there was too much absenteeism.

In 1920, both the church school and the Market Road school came under the auspices of the Essex Education Authority.

The Rev. F.D. Dormer-Pierce

The Rev. Francis Dormer-Pierce served as rector of Wickford from 1899 to 1908. He took a lively interest in village affairs, becoming chairman of the School Board and the Parish Council. His last meeting as chairman of the Parish Council was held on 12 March 1907. Mr Heslop remarked that the meeting felt deeply grateful to the rector for the 'able, genial and kindly' way in which he had acted as chairman. When the reverend finally left Wickford in 1908 to take up the incumbency of St John's in Southend, Mr Heslop proposed a vote of thanks to him for the 'able and impartial manner he always conducted the business of the Council and for the active part he had always taken in the interest and welfare of the parish'.

In the week before the Rev. Dormer-Pierce left the town, a farewell party was held for him at the public hall. A public subscription enabled the purchase of a framed farewell address with a picture of the rectory at the top and a

135 Broadway shops, c.1934.

view of St Catherine's at the foot, signed by 137 parishioners. In addition, the rector was presented with two solid silver candlesticks. Speakers averred that the rector and his wife had won the universal respect and esteem of the parishioners and they were thanked for the 'greatest interest always shown and the many services cheerfully rendered'. The Rev. Dormer-Pierce replied that he had made some of the best friends he had ever had in Wickford and that he had never known a dull moment there.

First World War

At the beginning of the First World War, the population of Wickford was around one thousand. A Cadet Corps was formed in the town and regular rifle practices were arranged, while money was collected to provide gifts for servicemen overseas and for the Belgian Relief Fund. When convoys of soldiers travelled through the town, villagers would come out and distribute tea and cigarettes. Wickford's

schoolchildren knitted socks and mittens and sewed handkerchiefs for the troops abroad.

On 30 May 1915, the 1st Herefordshire Regiment arrived at Wickford, under the command of Major R.H. Symonds-Taylor, and was billeted in local homes. St Catherine's parish magazine recorded: 'The parish has been greatly enlivened by the presence of the soldiers now billeted amongst us.' Among the benefits to the

136 Armed forces in the Broadway. These may be members of the 1st Herefordshire Regiment who were stationed in the town from May to July 1915.

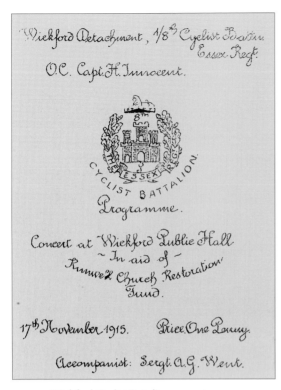

137 Wickford Cyclist Battalion concert programme, in aid of Runwell church. Two weeks later, the battalion staged another concert to raise money for Christmas presents for Downham men serving abroad.

138 Nevendon Bridge, 1915. This postcard was sent home to Master Sidney Law in Surrey from his father then serving in Wickford. 'We have very heavy days,' he wrote. 'Get up at 6 and work until 6.30, then sometimes march or rifle practice.'

locals were concerts given on the cricket field by the soldiers' band on Sunday afternoons. In return, a public subscription paid for the hire of the Public Hall, including use of a piano and caretaker at a cost of 25 shilling a week, for the benefit of the soldiers. When Major Symonds-Taylor left Wickford two months later, he wrote to the rector: 'I should personally like to thank most gratefully all these kind friends who have so generously provided amusements and entertainments for us; the free use of the Public Hall, the cricket field, the games and concerts so kindly arranged for us have all added very much to the pleasure of our visit …'.

The military again became a notable presence in the town in 1916 when they occupied the Congregational Chapel, paying £15 10s. for the privilege.

On the night of 28 January 1918, the first German Gotha bomber to be shot down at night over England was destroyed by Sopwith Camels from no.44 Squadron over Wickford. The plane fell near Castledon Road and represented the first unqualified victory in combat between aircraft flying at night. Not long afterwards, on 7 March, two British aeroplanes collided at Shotgate, killing both pilots, and a propeller was later set up on the site as a memorial.

At the end of the war, Welcome Home celebrations were held in the Public Hall – but 29 members of Wickford's armed forces did not return.

A meeting of parishioners unanimously decided that the war memorial should take the form of a cottage hospital, in view of the large number of men who went to defend their country. The Chairman of the War Memorial Committee, J.F. McLeod, reported that, as so many men had made the supreme sacrifice, it was the bounden duty of the town to raise a memorial that would at the same time show how deep was the town's appreciation for all they had so nobly done and be of service to the district. In the event, however, the parish purchased a bungalow in Southend Road for use as a nurses' home to stand as a memorial to

139 Inglenook, 1914. Wickford children photographed as war was declared.

the fallen of Wickford; Lord Lambourne, Lord Lieutenant of Essex, performed the opening ceremony. An annual Armistice Day parade was held from St Andrew's, culminating in the laying of wreaths on the nurses' home doorstep. The home was demolished in 1979 to make way for road building and the marble memorials were removed to Memorial Park.

During the war, agricultural labourers' wages were fixed at 32 shillings for 48 hours a week during winter and the same 32 shillings for 54 hours during summer. The ethic of home ownership continued to be encouraged by the government and Wickford's population continued to grow.

Inter-war development

In 1920, Wickford was described as a market town 'situated amidst pleasant rural surroundings'. For a short time it became

140 Nurses Home war memorial, 31 Southend Road. The building was demolished in 1976 to make way for the by-pass.

a minor tourist area, visited by Londoners in search of the countryside and by coach tours to the area from Southend, which also took in Battlesbridge, Nevendon and Benfleet woods. However, locals complained about the number of Sunday charabancs bringing summer visitors; traffic noise even interrupted services

ERECTED

TO THE HONOURED MEMORY OF THE FOLLOWING
LOCAL MEN WHO FOUGHT AND DIED IN THE
GREAT WAR 1914 – 1918 AND ALSO AS A
TOKEN OF GRATITUDE TO ALL WHO SERVED IN
THE SAME JUST CAUSE.

BUILT WITH THEIR LIVES AND DIED THAT LIFE MIGHT LIVE

141 First World War memorial marble, transferred to Memorial Park when the Nurses Home was demolished in 1976.

in the Congregational Chapel, then in the High Street. In 1922 a bye-law was proposed for the Basildon area preventing occupants of visiting charabancs from 'blowing horns, making loud singing or outcry or throwing money to be scrambled for whilst passing through a settlement in a manner which annoys the residents'.

By 1921, the population of Wickford was 1,413 (ecclesiastical parish) or 1,475 (civil parish). A downturn in cereal prices during the 1920s saw an increase in chicken farming and there were two manufacturers of poultry farming equipment in Wickford. Hall-Mark Hatcheries was founded in Wickford in the 1930s and became one of the largest international producers of day-old chicks, and manufacturers of poultry houses and equipment. An Essex Young Farmers Club started at Wickford County School in March 1932 and, after a

hiatus, was re-launched in October 1950 at Runwell Youth Centre. Despite this, there was a noticeable move away from agriculture and the 1920s-30s saw a further surge in town development, with Londoners increasingly keen to leave the city and find a peaceful country home. London firm Homesteads Ltd began marketing sites across the Home Counties, including at Brentwood and Wickford, seeking to attract ex-servicemen as smallholders or commuters.

James Gigney had made good use of the plots of Stileman's land he had purchased in 1906. The cottages not sold outright had been rented out for five to six shillings per week to the ordinary men and women who came to live and work in Wickford. However, in May 1920, Gigney decided to realise his investment and put much of the property up for sale. The auction, held at the Public Hall, comprised 21 lots, including Hall Cottages in Jersey Gardens, Victoria Terrace in Elm Road and Victoria Terrace in Swan Lane, plus Gigney's own grocery store fronting the Broadway which he had been leasing to Messrs Schofield and Martin since 1916. 'Rylands' in the London Road was sold by private treaty before the auction.

Croft House, described as a brick-built, double-fronted detached residence with four bedrooms, was again for sale with a sitting tenant, Thomas Darby, who was paying £34 per annum.

The pump in the High Street from which residents still obtained water was not included in the sale as it belonged to the parish, but it was finally dismantled in 1928.

In 1921, the governors of St Bartholomew's Hospital sold all their land in the area, including Friern Farm just east of Castledon Road. The estate continued to be farmed until it was sold as building land by Fred Taylor in 1933-4. Friern farmhouse itself plus its barns, slaughterhouse and two pieces of land still under requisition by the Ministry of Agriculture, Fisheries and Food was sold for development in 1945.

An auction at the *Castle* in May 1923 included the sale of 16 acres of glebe land, recently purchased from the Ecclesiastical Commissioners and divided into plots by a developer. The land was described as pleasantly situated on the 'highest and best' part of Wickford.

In 1921, the area now known as Shotgate came into the possession of the Archer family of Shot Farm. At that time the area was still farmland, partly in Wickford parish and partly in the parish of North Benfleet. Barns and cattle sheds stood at the corner of the present Fourth Avenue, while Fanton Chase was a cart track along which loaded wagons lumbered to Battlesbridge Mill.

In 1927, the Archer family sold the estate for residential development, and a vote was held at the *Swan Inn* as to whether Shotgate should become part of Wickford. The estate was originally planned with five avenues leading off Bruce Grove, which, before the development of the industrial area, had been intended to follow the line of the railway. The first residents of the estate were Mr and Mrs Wade who purchased a bungalow in Fifth Avenue, with their in-laws next door, Mr and Mrs Wheeler. The parade of shops was not an immediate success and the builder went bankrupt. Commuters from Shotgate, having to negotiate the unmade roads of the development, would leave their wellington boots with Mrs Richardson the newsagent and then catch the bus, for one penny, to the railway station. When Dr Campbell made house calls, he left his car in the main road, donned his wellington boots and walked up to the house.

Shot Farm itself (the former Great Aimes) was sold in June 1929 with 102 acres of productive farmland. The brick and timber farmhouse was, at that time, divided into two parts, each occupied by farm tenants.

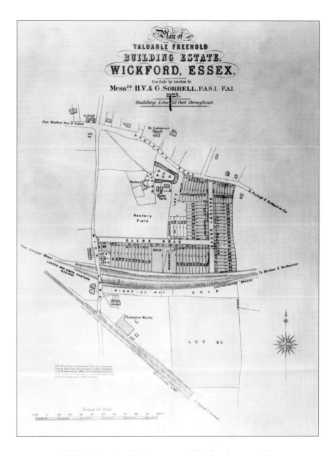

142 Glebe Farm building estate. This land was sold for development in 1923. Lots 3 and 4 are the glebe cottages built in 1907.

Local Roman Catholics bought 1½ acres of land from the Bridge House Farm Estate in 1924 and built themselves a church. Similarly, the Methodists built their first church in Southend Road in the late 1920s. In contrast, by 1929, the 48 acres of Church of England glebe land had been reduced to 10 acres.

In 1927, the headmaster of the Market Road school, Henry Kitson, recorded that over 400 children had been admitted in two years, with the comment: 'The migratory character of the population makes it very difficult to follow a definite scheme of instruction.' This suggests that many were still using Wickford as a holiday or seasonal retreat rather than making a permanent settlement here.

143 Wick Drive and the River Crouch.

In 1928, the Parish Council enrolled ten members into a voluntary fire brigade, with Mr F. Plantin as captain, and purchased a secondhand fire engine from the Thurrock brigade for £55. Their first call was to a haystack fire.

However, by 1930 the Parish Council was in disagreement with the brigade, who wanted to become independent.

Led by Eric Hassenruch, the Baptists established their own church in Bruce Grove in the 1930s, with a tin roof, electricity supplied by meter and a stove that was notoriously smokey. It was replaced with a permanent stone building in 1961. The Mission Hall on the London Road was replaced by a new church building dedicated to St Andrew in 1935, its first rector being the Rev. A.G. Munson. This church was redeveloped in 1964 with a new building dedicated by the Bishop of Chelmsford and incorporating the Good Shepherd window from the original mission hall. St Andrew's was promoted to the status of full parish church in 1980 when the Team Parish of Wickford and Runwell was formed,

144   Coal delivery in the High Street, *c.*1930.

145 Site of cinema, High Street. This lovely old cottage and the buildings in Fig.146 made way for the Carlton Cinema in 1937.

146 Percival Selby started his printing business in this shed in 1927 and later opened a second shop on the Broadway.

and was consecrated by the Bishop of Bradwell on 10 December 1981.

A new bridge between Runwell and Wickford was opened in the 1930s and a new Nevendon Road bridge was built in 1935. The local Ratepayers Association actively campaigned for Wickford to become separate from Billericay Rural District Council, while the local Farmers Union, which met at the *Castle*, was one of the biggest in Essex. In 1934 Billericay Rural District Council became

the Billericay Urban District Council, which prompted calls for Wickford to join Rayleigh Rural District as residents still saw their town as predominantly a rural area.

The Wickford library opened in 1932. In 1933, the Public Hall was used as a classroom because of excessive overcrowding at the schools, and in 1937 Wickford County Senior School opened opposite the council school in Market Road. It had ten classrooms and an assembly hall built from local brick, all at a cost of

147 Shotgate Corner with a Campbell's bus. A public vote was held at the *Swan* in 1927 as to whether Shotgate should become part of Wickford.

£14,985. The headmaster was Mr F.W. Rose. In 1959 this building became Wickford Junior School, while the original school became infants only and senior pupils relocated to the new Beauchamps High School.

The End of Wickford Hall

Wickford Hall, described as a 'picturesque country residence' with four reception rooms, six bedrooms and three acres of gardens, was offered for sale by auction on 8 May 1926 at Southend. Water was laid to the house

148 Eastern National advertisement for bus and coach services from Wickford.

and it was lit by gas, but not connected to the electricity or main sewer. Lot One, the auctioneers suggested, was 'particularly suitable for a city man'.

Lot 2 in the sale was Wickford Hall Farm, an 'excellent dairy farm' of 74 acres of good pasture and arable land with a dwelling house, extensive farm buildings and a pair of brick-built cottages. The purchaser was obliged to pay an additional cost for the crops and farm machinery.

A section of the estate fronting the Southend Road was offered separately as a 20-acre building site, with the incentive that Liverpool Street station was a mere 50 minutes by rail and Southend only 20 minutes. The sewer, potential buyers were assured, was laid in the main road near the entrance to the farm and connection could easily be made on payment of the local authority charge. The electric light main also passed the property.

The farm was sold for £2,200 but Wickford Hall was withdrawn from the sale and re-marketed in May 1929.

Cinema

Local man Walter French built the Carlton Cinema in 1937 in the High Street on the site of the thatched cottage often seen in old picture postcards of Wickford. By 1945 it was owned by Mr B.E. Fortesque as part of his Radian circuit. The cinema closed in the mid-1950s and Woolworths moved in, demolishing the cinema building in the early 1970s and replacing it with a modern store on the site.

After the closure of the Carlton, Wickford's Public Hall in Jersey Gardens opened as a cinema in 1955 under the name The Astoria. However, it was barely open a year before it closed again. The building then underwent many changes of use, including a gym in the 1990s.

Public Transport

The A127 London to Southend road reached Basildon in 1924 and was completed as far as Southend in 1927, greatly improving east-west communications. However, a Ministry of Transport survey in 1937 commented that north-south transport routes in the area were 'little better than tortuous country lanes'.

The Campbell family of Pitsea ran a horse-drawn vehicle to Wickford from about 1900 and later introduced a motor bus service. In 1913 there was some concern about the speed of traffic in the village and a 12mph limit was introduced for cars travelling through. However, a proposed motor bus service to Southend could not start immediately because the roads were not good enough to support large vehicles. The first regular bus service, run by the Westcliff Motor Service Ltd, didn't begin until the 1920s.

In July 1933, the City Coach Company acquired an interest in the New Empress Saloons company which had operated the London to Southend bus service since 1928. Buses ran every 15 minutes from Market Road, Wickford to Shotgate, at a cost of one penny per adult. In 1953, the City Coach Company was nationalised and became part

149 Coronation celebration programme, 1937.

of the Westcliff Motor Services, later absorbed by Eastern National.

National Coaches, which eventually became Eastern National, ran services through Wickford from at least 1925. On Fridays it operated a special service from Grays to Wickford, and ran buses from Benfleet on Mondays for the market.

Pattens Coaches, which had a garage in the Runwell Road, Amon & Davies of Ramsden Heath and the Wickford Carriage Company were all taken over by Eastern National in the 1930s. Other local companies absorbed by Eastern National during the 1950s were Old Tom's Motor Services from Brentwood and Campbells of Pitsea. Despite these numerous services, cycling remained a very popular form of transport.

Ten

Towards the Twenty-First Century

Second World War

The face of Wickford was transformed by the advent of the Second World War with, for example, a machine-gun emplacement in the London Road and the fire brigade moving from a site at the south of the High Street to take over poultry sheds nearby. Concrete posts were set into the London Road to obstruct enemy tanks in case of invasion and Shotgate was surrounded by tank traps and blockhouses. Local police officer Sgt Brewer organised the requisition of all privately owned weapons and two battalions of Home Guard were formed. Volunteers included Col Henry Burton, Sudbury's 62-year-old MP, and 19-year-old Thomas Frew, a medical student who later took over his father's Wickford GP practice. A

150 Sergeant Brewer, centre, was Wickford's resident police officer during the Second World War.

camp for Italian prisoners of war was established on Nevendon Road, the prisoners being put to work on local farms. The Black Watch and Highland Light Infantry were billeted in the town, either with local families or in empty houses.

Wickford's situation on the route between Germany and London was obviously of concern – German bombers returning from London would use the railway line and A127 as guidelines for their flight path.

A British fighter plane crashed in Castledon Road in August 1940 and another in Fanton Chase later the same month. In September 1940, an enemy aircraft ME110 was brought down over DeBeavoirs Farm, while British planes fell at Nevendon and Cranfield Park Road. Youngsters would scour the fields looking for souvenirs from fallen aircraft.

On 22 January 1944, a Dornier 217M1 was caught by AA artillery over Pitsea and crashed at Runwell Hospital, while on 10 February 1945 a rocket fell about 20 yards from the railway line at Wickford, severing all telephone and control communications and blocking both lines with debris. All trains were stopped for two hours.

Newspapers reported that the Wickford district had been 'harassed from bombing by almost every type of bomb the Nazis have'. For example, eight high explosive bombs, familiar between May 1940 and February 1944, fell on Wickford Senior School in April 1943. Parachute mines fell in Swan Lane, Elder Avenue and

151 Wartime special policemen, led by Cultivation Officer Sergeant Holland.

152 Samuel and Ethel Wright of the Wickford fire service, 1943. Ethel was the first female member of the brigade.

London Road during 1940, while fly bombs fell in Wick Drive in August 1944. Incendiary bombs fell between 1940-44, including two on Wickford railway station and a canister of 1,000 bombs on Wick Farm. During late 1944 to early 1945, long range bombs hit Shotgate on five separate occasions. Oil bombs fell on three occasions during 1940, while phosphorus bombs fell near the town centre in April 1943 and February 1944.

War stories ranged from the unfortunate – Mr Raven's allotment was destroyed by a 44ft-wide crater; to the triumphant – Mrs V. Marsh and her son were dug out of their Anderson shelter unscathed when their bungalow received a direct hit; to the tragic – Mr and Mrs Pratt and their daughter Molly all died when their Swan Lane home was hit by an incendiary bomb.

The Red Cross sales for the Essex Agricultural Fund were a major contribution by Essex farmers to the war effort. Across the county the Farmers Union organised auctions in the cattle markets, with farmers donating livestock and contributions of bottles of whisky, etc. made by local tradesmen. Auctioneers gave their services free, while farmers' wives ran sales of produce, teas, flags and raffle tickets. In 1943, the Wickford appeal, in a joint effort with Chelmsford, collected £3,000.

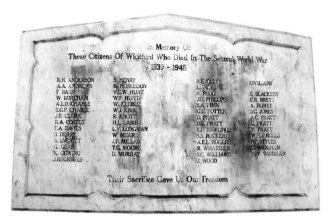

153 Second World War memorial marble, transferred from the Nurses Home to Wickford Memorial Park in 1976.

Agricultural Committees were set up to maximise agricultural production, including the clearance and rehabilitation of thousands of acres of land. These bureaucratic bodies were, unsurprisingly, unpopular with local people. In addition, Essex County Council appointed District Organisers under the Institute of Agriculture. These organisers were commissioned to co-ordinate events for the instruction

of farmers and labourers. H.E. Nichols was appointed District Organiser of Wickford and neighbouring districts in south Essex. However, a few months after his appointment, Mr Nichols was mistaken for a German airman by an enthusiastic member of the Home Guard; he was shot in the stomach and died.

The war brought about an end to plotland development and land not yet sold returned to agriculture for the duration. However, flimsy structures intended only as holiday cottages often became permanent homes for families bombed out of London and many weekend shacks were commandeered to house East End refugees.

Despite its location, and the orange glow from blitzed London being visible from the town, Wickford became a temporary home for evacuees. Children stayed at the Market Road school before being allocated to local families.

At Market Road, some lessons were taught in the three brick-built air-raid shelters provided with space for 300. School railings were taken for the war effort and, in 1941,

154　Hall's Corner, 1955. Compare this with the view on page 47.

a first-aid post was set up nearby. The Home Guard used the playground for evening drill practice and soldiers were stationed in the fields nearby. These troops left Wickford in May 1944 and took part in the D-Day landings.

Post-War Development

Despite the land sales in the early years of the 20th century, Arthur Mee was still moved to describe Wickford as 'a compact village' in 1940. For those unable to return to London after the war, an estate of prefabricated houses was erected east of Nevendon Road to provide temporary homes, and housing development, temporarily halted by the war, gained momentum, steadily increasing the bounds of the town.

After the war, the government, seeking to house many former London residents made homeless by the war, identified the tiny hamlet of Basildon south of Wickford as an ideal location for a new town. The proposal was also seen as a means of addressing the problems created by plotland developments, described by Essex County Council as 'uncontrolled developments of sub-standard housing with poor or non-existent services'.

The Basildon Development Corporation came into being in 1949 with a remit to build a new town on the site of the village of Basildon to accommodate 50,000 people. The development was to have far-reaching effects on Wickford, transforming it from a remote village into an urban suburb almost overnight. On 1 April 1955, the Billericay Urban District Council became the Basildon Urban District Council, with an area of 27,139 acres, taking in both Billericay and Wickford, along with other small villages.

However, while the Pitsea and Laindon plotlands were effectively swallowed up by Basildon New Town, substantial semi-developed plotland areas remained in the Wickford area for several years.

During the 1950s, Wickford High Street was redeveloped with the building of more retail premises; Memorial Park was given a bowling green and tennis courts, and roads were made up. It was suggested that Wickford centre be urbanised to concentrate development and arrest its spread. This followed recommendation in the 1944 Abercrombie Report which had suggested 'a complete cessation of all building outside a tightly drawn line round the central core, the acquisition by the Housing Authority of the vacant plots within this line and the erection by them of substantially-built houses on a proportion of these sites'. Owners of plots outside the designated area would be offered alternative plots or dwellings within the central area and the land returned to agriculture. This was incorporated into the Essex County Council Development Plan, approved in 1957. As pressure for housing increased, the plan was amended to make all the plotland areas subject to greenbelt restrictions.

After the Second World War, the system of marketing agricultural produce gradually changed, with more animals going directly to abattoir and meat processing premises, and the livestock pens at Wickford market were replaced by stalls of produce and household goods. During the 1950s and '60s, Essex Farmers Unions amalgamated as transport allowed greater distances to be travelled. Wickford combined with the South East Essex branch to cover an area from Rochford to Epping. By 1990, the National Farmers Union had adopted a policy of regionalisation, resulting in an eastern region embracing seven counties.

During the 1950s, whist drives, fêtes and sales were organised to raise money towards a public hall for local entertainment for residents of Shotgate. £1,200 was raised, with grants from the Ministry of Education bringing the total to £2,418. A plot of land in Bruce Grove was purchased from Basildon Urban District Council at a cost of £325 and Councillor

Tanswell, Chairman of Basildon Council, officially opened the hall on 8 November 1958. The wooden wall panelling was reclaimed from an East End pub, the flooring had first seen service in American pre-fab buildings and the doors were rescued from a scrap yard, but Mr Day of the Essex County Council Education Department said that he had 'never seen a better community hall than the one at Shotgate'.

The industrial estate at the end of Bruce Grove replaced a chicken farm owned by Chase Cross Bakeries, and the first factory to open on the industrial estate was Poulton, Self & Lee. In 1961, a permanent stone building replaced the tin-roofed hall that had served as Shotgate's Baptist church for many years, depriving subsequent generations of the experience of enjoying a service in a room filled with smoke from a wood stove.

The railway line was electrified by the end of 1956, and in 1967 Wickford station, in common with all those from Billericay to Southend, ceased to handle goods traffic.

The Great Flood

Wickford was no stranger to flooding, with water up to a depth of a foot or more a regular occurrence since the earliest times; the London Road at its junction with the High Street, and the High Street at its junction with the Southend Road were often impassable. Raised footways for pedestrians had been one of the first projects undertaken by the Wickford Parish Council and people were commonly known to have taken their animals, including pigs and chickens, into the upper storeys of their homes to avoid the flood waters. In the early 1950s, the River Crouch was given a concrete culvert for that section of its course through Wickford, which minimised the problem of regular flooding. However, in 1953, the Great Tide so disastrous to Essex coastal towns was also felt in Wickford where the Crouch once again burst its banks.

Wickford's worst flood, however, came about on 5 September 1958 when hours of heavy rain turned the River Crouch into a raging torrent and a wall of floodwater raced through Wickford town centre. The water rushed down Southend, Runwell and London Roads, inundating the town to a degree unknown within living memory. At Halls Corner, the lowest part of the town, the water reached six feet deep. The disaster made national news headlines and led the *News of the World* to describe Wickford as 'gumboot alley'. Thousands of pounds worth of damage was done to shops and homes; vehicles were totally submerged and furniture and personal items floated out of shops and homes.

The High Street was effectively cut off from the outside world and 16 people were stranded all night on top of a double-decker bus. After an uncomfortable night, the passengers were rescued at 9a.m. by Mr S. Carter in his former army DKUW, an amphibious vehicle. They were taken to the Salvation Army hall where emergency bedding and food had been provided for more than 100 people who had left their homes during the night. Others, many rescued by firemen and policemen in a flotilla of small boats, had been given refuge at Market Road School. By morning swathes of countryside was still under water; in the town cars and buses lay abandoned.

The village was left without electricity for several days afterwards and, although trains started running as soon as the waters began to subside, passengers had to walk across sodden fields and along part of the track to reach the station.

The flood proved disastrous for local farmers. The fields, already saturated by heavy summer rainfall, became swamps and any crops had to be abandoned where they grew. Barns were flooded, corn stacks stood in three feet of water, potatoes were washed out of the ground and the poultry losses were considerable. The *Essex Farmers' Journal* reported:

155 Many people were stranded in their upstairs rooms for days after severe flooding in September 1958.

156 This truck forged through the floodwaters, creating a huge wave that burst into the nearby newsagent's and knocked Barrie Adcock off his feet.

157 Floodwater stood deepest at Halls Corner, one of the lowest points in the town. Sixteen people were stranded all night on this bus, the 251 service from Wood Green, London.

158 Railway bridge, September 1958. It took months to recover from the physical damage of the floods – the financial costs were felt by shopkeepers and farmers for years.

159   Aerial view of Runwell Road, September 1958. Notice the Memorial Park gates, centre top.

At one farm near Wickford, 3.27 inches were measured in 90 minutes, and we've heard one suggestion of 3½ inches. To get it into any sort of perspective, you have to think of a month's normal rainfall in Essex coming down within an hour.

It took months to clean up the town and years for local businesses to recoup their losses.

Subsequently, the course of the River Crouch was altered, and its banks were concreted during the 1960s. However, flooding occurred again on 14-15 September 1968 during a storm that also caused lightning damage to the railway between Wickford and Rayleigh.

During July 1976, fierce thunderstorms brought an inch of rain in two hours. The Southend Road at Wickford was under four feet of water and many homes suffered a power cut.

Urban Developments

In 1959, a new fire station was built on the Nevendon Road. In the same year, Beauchamps School opened as a secondary school, followed by Hilltop Junior School (1967), Castledon Special School (1969), Grange Primary School (1969), Barn Hall Primary School (1970), Hill Top Infant School (1972), Bromfords Comprehensive School (1973), North Crescent Primary School and Grange Infants School (1973).

160   Castledon Road.

In September 1960, the Diocese of Chelmsford applied to the Queen for an alteration to Wickford's parish boundaries. They proposed that all those parts of the parish of Downham, Ramsden Bellhouse, Runwell and South Hanningfield, that were adjacent to Wickford and remote from their 'home' parishes, be annexed to Wickford. Less than one month later, the Privy Council officially approved the scheme.

The community centre opened in Market Road in October 1963.

The 1964 Wickford Development Plan stated that the area:

> consists of poor quality land which has progressively gone out of cultivation over 60 years. Prior to 1914, numerous plots were laid out at low density. They lacked essential public services and fronted unmade roads. Many of these roads have since disappeared. Scattered residential development, mainly substandard in size, accommodation or materials, took place before 1939 on a small proportion of plots. Much of the remaining land is unused and affected by spreading scrub. Some ownerships are confused or unknown.

The Council subsequently adopted a one-for-one replacement of plotland houses, as a result of a growing number of planning appeals.

In the late 1960s, the Basildon Urban District Council drew up plans for further redevelopment of Wickford town centre. They proposed a new north-south major traffic route east of the High Street, while Irvon Lane would provide access to Market Road and the west side of the High Street. The High Street would then be closed to vehicles and a market square developed, while the Broadway would be restricted to public buses and become 'a pleasant and safe precinct'.

The plans were the subject of study by a focus group led by F. Davies of the Shotgate Community Association. The group described 1960s Wickford, then home to some 22,000 people, as 'undeniably and boringly urban', and suggested that drastic action was required to give the town coherence and pride in itself.

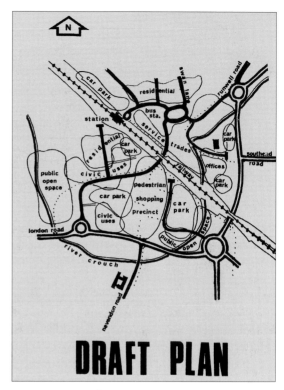

161 1960s draft development plan. At this stage, it was proposed to pedestrianise the High Street.

Following these consultations, several old buildings in the High Street were taken down to make way for modernisation which included the Willowdale Centre, opened in 1973. A new police station was built in London Road in 1966 and 1972 saw the demolition of the High Street Congregational Chapel. The

162 Southend Road post office, *c.*1960.

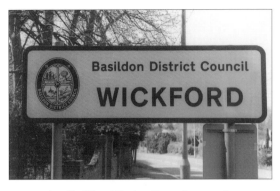

163   Basildon District Council town sign.

Methodists united with the Congregationalists in 1969 and the modern Christ Church was completed in 1974. The Rev. Stanley Hodge was the first resident minister of the united church. The original Methodist Church, built in Southend Road in 1927, was demolished in 1984.

In 1974, the boroughs, rural and urban districts that comprised Essex were consolidated into 14 district councils. Central government produced a Strategic Plan identifying south Essex as a major growth area, and Wickford continued to grow as an urban area.

In 1975, Basildon Council purchased 'Rylands' on the corner of Nevendon Road for use as an Area Office. This had been the home of Dr Craig Campbell in the 1930s-40s.

Soon afterwards, increasing traffic through the town, congestion in the High Street and a need for rapid access to the A127 and Basildon resulted in the decision to build a Wickford by-pass. Work began in 1976 and included another railway bridge and a large roundabout east of the town centre and necessitated the demolition of the nurses home. David Fisher, the County Highway Chief, officially opened the by-pass in August 1979. The Southend Road was effectively cut in two, and Wickford Bridge, marking the crossing point on the River Crouch that had led to the initial development of settlement on the site, lost its position as the focal point of the town.

Between 1970-79, 16 per cent of families moving into the Basildon district settled in Wickford; most of these people came from east London or other parts of Essex. In 1979, Wickford's population was 22,343 people.

164   Aerial view of High Street, taken soon after the by-pass opened in 1979.

165 The *Castle Inn*, photographed in 1998 just before it was demolished and the site taken over by a supermarket. Note how the doorway had moved from the centre to the end of the building.

By the end of the 20th century, Wickford had become a small manufacturing centre, although predominantly characterised as a commuter town, with 50 per cent of the adult male population employed in London. For their benefit, the railway station was largely rebuilt in 1980. However, the modernisation of Wickford town centre has often entailed the destruction of its links with the past. For example, shopping facilities expanded with the opening of the Ladygate shopping mall in 1982, built on the site of Ladybrow, for many years the home of Dr Robert Frew who had worked in the town for 50 years. Similarly, the 300-year-old *Castle Hotel* was demolished in 1998 and replaced by an Aldi supermarket.

The 21st century promises to see a new incarnation of Wickford with further development of the town centre but it is hoped that, while moving forward, Wickford does not forget its past.

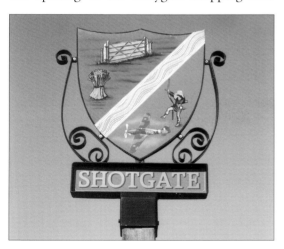

166 Shotgate village sign includes a gate, a sheaf for their farming heritage, the waters of the River Crouch, an archer for the Archer family and a Spitfire to commemorate the area's involvement in the Second World War.

167 Wickford town sign was designed by residents in the 1960s, depicting the seaxes of Essex and a sheaf and scythe to represent the agricultural heritage of the town.

Select Bibliography

Basildon Urban District Council, *Wickford Town Centre* (1980)

Booker, J.M.L., *The Essex Turnpike Trusts* (1979)

Collins, Andrew, *The Running Well Mystery* (1983)

Currie, Ian, Davison, Mark and Ogley, Bob, *The Essex Weather Book* (1992)

Dormer-Pierce, Rev. F., *Notes on the Parish of Wickford* (1905)

Gigney, J., *Old Wickford as I Knew It* (1935)

Grimwood, Bob, *The Cinemas of Essex* (1995)

Hall, Peter, *Images of England, Wickford* (1996)

Hardy, D. and Ward, C., *Arcadia for All* (1984)

Horn, Pamela, *The Changing Countryside* (1984)

Morant, P., *The History and Antiquities of the County of Essex* 1760-68 (1978)

Prance, David and Feldwick, Lesley, *History and Guide of St Catherine's Church* (2000)

Wakeham, M., *Aspects of Wickford History* (1982)

Wakeham, M., *Wickford Memories* (1983)

Ward, Sadie, *Seasons of Change* (1982)

Wormell, Peter, *Essex Farming* 1900-2000 (2000)

Index

References which relate to illustrations only are given in **bold**.